The Sweet Kitchen

The Sweet Kitchen

Tales and Recipes of India's Favourite Desserts

Rajyasree Sen

ALEPH

ALEPH BOOK COMPANY
An independent publishing firm
promoted by *Rupa Publications India*

First published in India in 2022
by Aleph Book Company
7/16 Ansari Road, Daryaganj
New Delhi 110 002

Copyright © Rajyasree Sen 2022

All rights reserved.

The author has asserted her moral rights.

The views and opinions expressed in this book are those of the author and the facts are as reported by her, which have been verified to the extent possible, and the publisher is not in any way liable for the same.

Cover illustration of spices: iStock/FingerMedium

No part of this publication may be reproduced, transmitted, or stored in a retrieval system, in any form or by any means, without permission in writing from Aleph Book Company.

ISBN: 978-93-91047-72-6

1 3 5 7 9 10 8 6 4 2

This book is sold subject to the condition that it shall not, by way of trade or otherwise, be lent, resold, hired out, or otherwise circulated without the publisher's prior consent in any form of binding or cover other than that in which it is published.

*To my little hounds—Goebbels, Mendel, and Chotu,
who were the perfect writing companions.*

Contents

Introduction	1
Sandesh: Muse of the Bengal Renaissance	7
Rosogolla: Who Stole My Cheese?	17
The Christmas Cake: Culture Chameleon	27
Payasam, Payesh, Kheer: The Three Avatars of Sweet Pudding	35
Halwa: The Arab Who Strayed onto the Indian Palate	44
Barfi: When Art Outdoes Nature	51
Gulab Jamun: Everybody's Celebration Sweetmeat	59
Jalebi: Sweet Lord of the Rings	66
Daulat Ki Chaat: The Lingering Taste of Old Delhi	71

Mishti Doi, Shrikhand, Bhapa Doi: Haute Culture Curd	79
Goan Sweets: Gems from an Indigenous Pastelaria	86
Firinghee Sweets: Delicious Relics of the Raj	97
In God's Name: Sweetmeats and Cultural Congeniality	106
Acknowledgments	116
Recommended Reading	118

Introduction

In India, sweets are a satisfying finale to even a less-than-sumptuous meal. We eat sweets to commemorate every occasion, joyful or otherwise. In fact, sweets and desserts are as ubiquitous and diverse in India as its household gods. It's also Indian sweets that seem to break down the barriers between communities, and are savoured and enjoyed across the country without a pause or even a passing thought as to where they originated from. In today's political climate, there are few moments as satisfying as seeing Hindus crave some creamy sheer korma during Eid, or Punjabis asking their Bengali friends and acquaintances for mishti doi. The fact that Muslim cooks bake the Christmas cake in Calcutta (no, I will not refer to it as Kolkata) for a largely Hindu clientele to celebrate a Christian festival proves that when it comes to desserts and mithai, suddenly—and maybe conveniently—the barriers drop away. This, to me, is one of the biggest reasons to celebrate the sweets of India.

As a Bengali who grew up in Calcutta, I realized early on that the city and the Bengali identity were both synonymous with 'mishti' or sweets, almost as if the two were the last word in confectionary. It is, in fact, true that there isn't a street or a locality in Calcutta that doesn't boast of a sweetshop. Growing up, the city also made me realize that life began and ended with sweets—just as our meals did. Payesh, or rice cooked in sweetened milk, is the first spoon of solid food that a Bengali child tastes during annaprashan or the rice-feeding ceremony. Shraddhas and chauthas, the Hindu rituals of mourning, are not complete without a sweet dish—usually sandesh or barfi, depending on which part of India you're in. Every ritual and religious ceremony in India is marked by sweets specifically prepared for that occasion, such as the modak during Ganesh Chaturthi.

In India, going to someone's house almost always includes being offered something to eat and drink—something savoury will always be accompanied by something sweet—and not accepting it can be a sacrilegious act. The concept of 'muh meetha karo', which loosely translates to 'sweeten your palate', is a tradition and a sign of Indian hospitality which cannot be rebuffed regardless of whether you have a sweet tooth or not! I've visited homes in North India, where I've been offered a peda or a barfi or a laddoo. In Bengal, you'd be offered a sandesh or a rosogolla or a pantua. If any of these terms seem unfamiliar to you, you will acquaint yourself with them through the course of this book. For that is the aim of this book—to inform readers about sweets and sweet-making techniques, and to explore the cultural influences that led to the creation of various sweets considered quintessentially Indian today. I want to provide the reader with a richer, if not a sweeter, appreciation of the different communities residing in India and their relationship with the sweets they prepare and enjoy. And I hope that, as a result, the reader is inspired to taste local sweets while travelling or visiting friends.

Growing up, I was taught that when you visit a new city or a new country, you must always taste the local cuisine. I was even encouraged to visit local kitchens and observe the culinary habits and traditions of different cultures. Ingredients and cooking procedures, it was felt, provided a direct insight into the historical and cultural forces that shape a region and its people.

I must confess that I do not have an especially sweet tooth. Yet, in spite of the fact that I find many Indian sweets a little too treacly, I make it a point to taste every sweet offered to me, or anything that catches my eye. I always try to identify ingredients common to the parts of the country I travel to and to other sweets I am familiar with. This lifelong curiosity has led me to many questions: why does the payesh in Bengal sometimes not use rice? What makes kheer different from payasam? Is shrikhand the same as bhapa doi? Where did seviyan come from? Why do most communities not use yoghurt in their desserts? Why does Bengal alone use paneer or chhana in desserts? And, for that matter, when did we learn to make chhana? I have tried to understand why some regions use milk, while others use cottage cheese or jaggery as the main ingredient in all their sweets. Why is the same dish prepared differently by different communities? Why is dessert served at the beginning of a meal in one community, but at the end of a meal elsewhere?

As a result of extensive research, I have also discovered historical facts I was not aware of, or had not even considered. For instance, which desserts must we thank the Persians, the Mughals, the Portuguese, and the French for? While I knew that a sweet had been created for Lady Canning in Bengal, I had no idea which Mughal emperor to thank for bringing halwa to India, or the Sikh connection to the creation of the kaju barfi, or that you can, indeed, make sweets with meat and eggs in India. I have also tried to demystify the very controversial question of whether Bengal made the rosogolla first, or if the credit for that sweet spongey roundel of cottage cheese actually goes to Odisha. I have discovered that daulat ki chaat, an airy, churned milk dessert available only during the cold winters of North India, has a Mongol provenance. As someone who loves cooking and experimenting with new ingredients, I have included some tried-and-tested recipes in each chapter. I hope *The Sweet Kitchen* will introduce readers to a tasting menu of the innumerable sweets that define so many parts of India. I have tried to include sweets from every region, and hope that readers delve into the genesis of each sweet too, understanding how its location determines its ingredients, and acknowledging the historical and cultural influences which helped create it. I cannot claim that this is a definitive guide to all the sweets of India, but I hope this book is able to provide readers with a sufficient serving of anecdotes, history, and recipes to tickle their interests, if not their palates.

Sandesh
Muse of the Bengal Renaissance

'Mishti khaabe?' is invariably the question with which a guest is welcomed to a Bengali household, even one outside of Bengal. This rhetorical question is usually followed by the arrival of a quarter plate with something salty—a nimki or a thin-crust Bengali samosa called shingara—and a selection of sweets which are, more often than not, different types of sandesh. A staple of Bengali cuisine, sandesh is a mouth-watering delicacy made from sweetened cottage cheese, sometimes in a delicious union with date palm jaggery. Sandesh is, however, much more than the sum of its ingredients—invented at the height of the Bengal Renaissance, it was a symbol of cultural refinement and haute cuisine at the time, and subsequently, a cure for every discerning

Bengali's interminable craving for mishti in particular and for pre-siesta desserts in general.

No other state in India makes sandesh or any variant of this crumbly sweet. Nor has any other state ever laid claim to its creation. In fact, sandesh is so quintessentially Bengali that every ceremony and custom in Bengal includes some avatar of this delicacy. Often, as part of a bridal trousseau or totto, where it is customary to carry a fish dressed as a bride complete with saree and sindoor—here, the bride's family substitues the real McCoy with one made entirely of sandesh. This fish is made of chhanar sandesh, a sweetened cottage cheese, which is typically rolled into balls or flattened into small discs, and sometimes placed in moulds to resemble the shapes of fruit or shells similar to biscuit or tart moulds. This piscine sandesh, which can serve at least twenty to thirty people, is lovingly designed to resemble a real fish with its eyes, scales, and tail in their proper proportions.

The genius of the Bengali confectioners—both Hindu and Muslim—is most clearly visible in the impressive array of milk-based sweets that make up the repertoire of Bengali sweets.* A defining element in most of these sweets—from the sandesh to the rosogolla and rosomalai—is that they are made partly or wholly from the sweetened cottage cheese we know as chhana. The use of chhana is unique to Bengal, but before the eighteenth century, even in Bengal, sweets were generally made from evaporated milk or kheer, as in most parts of India

---

*Amer Wahab, 'A brief introduction to Bengal's gastronomic history', *Daily Star*, 24 February 2020.

The Sweet Kitchen

today. This erstwhile reluctance to use chhana can be traced back to the belief that 'cutting' milk with acid to make chhana is tantamount to sin.

Bengali sweets can be loosely divided into two categories: homemade sweets such as patishapta, naru, pithe, and payesh; and those that were created and perfected by Moiras in sweetshops, such as the chhana-based sweets, sandesh and rosogolla. It's important to understand the fine distinction between chhana and paneer. Chhana is the softer, crumblier version of paneer before the latter is pressed into its solid form. Popular folklore has it that sandesh was created by an enterprising milkman whose milk had curdled. Instead of throwing the milk away, he flavoured the solid part of the curdled milk with jaggery and divided the mixture into roundels. There is no way to check the veracity of this story, but it has been repeated often enough to make its way to the oral tradition that surrounds the mysterious origins and history of sandesh.

A more plausible story, however, concerns the early Portuguese settlers in Bengal, whose fondness for cottage cheese brought chhana to Bengali kitchens in the seventeenth century. Historically, the Portuguese were renowned confectioners, and their cheese and dessert making skills would have been an inspiration to Bengali confectioners. A large number of Portuguese men also married Bengali Muslim women—many of these women were accomplished cooks and confectioners themselves. The women, in turn, adopted Portuguese culinary practices which resulted in a new kind of sweetmeat making its appearance in the home via the kitchen or a local shop. In *Sweet Invention: A History of Dessert*, Michael Krondl mentions that the French physician and traveller François Bernier, who lived in India between 1659 and 1666, had observed that, 'Bengal likewise is celebrated for its sweetmeats, especially in places inhabited by the Portuguese, who are skillful in the art of preparing them and with whom they are an article of considerable trade.'[*] There is no question that Portuguese cheese influenced desserts in Bengal and neighbouring Odisha.

Sandesh was probably created by confectioners and sold commercially during the second half of the nineteenth century.[†] Till the mid-nineteenth century, there is no mention of a sandesh or rosogolla in recipe books or in literature. Although I have been told that the word 'sandesh' is mentioned in medieval Bengali literature, I have never been able to ascertain this. The word is also mentioned in *Chaitanyacharitamrita*, the biography of the fifteenth-century Bhakti saint Chaitanya, and in the fifteenth-century poet Krittibas Ojha's Ramayana, but whether the sandesh mentioned in these works is the same as the sandesh we eat today is unclear.[‡]

In Calcutta, the capital of West Bengal, it would not be an exaggeration to say that every street has a sweetshop and a chemist or two. The chemist usually keeps a stock of digestives that help fellow Bengalis survive until their next meal, after

---
[*]Michael Krondl, *Sweet Invention: A History of Dessert*, Chicago: Chicago Review Press, 2011.
[†]Wahab, 'A brief introduction to Bengal's gastronomic history'..
[‡]Asheesh Mamgain, 'Sandesh to Ledikeni (Named After Lady Canning) Delhi Does Bengali Sweets Proud', *The Citizen*, 26 September 2018.

which the whole process starts again. The first sweetshops in Calcutta mushroomed in the nineteenth century, and Bengalis immediately flocked to them. Moiras, who were known for sandesh, often inspired family cooks who hoped to replicate the fashionable dessert at home—but trust me, this is one of those sweetmeats that never tastes as good when made at home.

Which is why, even today, sandesh, pantua, and mishti doi are rarely made at home. These were created and perfected by Moiras in sweetshops. My grandmother, who was a stellar cook, and even our family cooks, who whipped up the most delicious Bengali dishes, never wasted time making sandesh since you could always purchase the very best of sandesh at the neighbourhood mishtir dokaan.

Even today, you can see Moiras sitting in the small sweetshops, wearing just a lungi or a dhoti folded above their knees, bare chested, and with a prominent paunch (a work hazard), leaning over a big dekchi of oil, frying shingaras and jilipees, and wiping their brow with a checkered gamcha, which is usually draped over their shoulders.

In fact, the story of sandesh would not be complete without dwelling on the Moiras, the original creators of the sweet. As a testament to the all-consuming impact of sandesh and mishti on even the most evolved and intellectual of us, writer and musician Amit Chaudhuri's conceptual artworks, displayed as part of 'The Sweet Shop Owners of Calcutta and Other Ideas', provide a unique perspective on sweetshops in Renaissance-era Bengal. In it, Chaudhuri has photographed the proprietors of some of

Calcutta's most famous sweetshops—dressed in their kochaano dhuti-panjabi with Kashmiri shawls draped over their shoulders. These men—skilled entrepreneurs and gourmands who set up famous shops such as KC Das and Ganguram's—nurtured Calcutta's love for mishti. These were also the men who hired the singularly talented cooks from the Moira community that eventually stirred up sweet-making traditions in Bengal.*

The Moiras have also played a critical role in Bengal's cultural reformation. Once Calcutta was named the capital of British India in 1833, it attracted thousands of people from neighbouring states and districts—artisans, landowners, and entrepreneurs. The Moiras migrated from the surrounding districts, especially Hooghly, and were part of this influx of migrants into the newly-minted capital. As is the case in India, caste determines what you do and where you do it. The world of sweets is no different. The Moiras were one of the original nine castes which made up Bengal's Nabasakha caste group—a group of occupation-based castes. But the sweet tooth bit through the caste barrier. As a result, even at a time when caste determined many social and dietary exclusions, the Moira community's social standing was quite elevated.

Krondl narrates how Bengali Brahmins, who never accepted food as gifts because they didn't want to inadvertently touch food that a lower-caste person might have cooked, happily accepted sandesh. Because what is caste in the face of a delicious crumbly

---

*Priyadarshini Chatterjee, 'Why the sandesh is the perfect representation of cultural reforms in nineteenth-century Calcutta', *Scroll.in*, 16 August 2018.

mouthful of sandesh? Another reason for the prominence of the Moira community in Bengal can be ascribed to the spread of Vaishnavism in Bengal in the pre-colonial era. The Vaishnavites worshipped Krishna who, as a pastoral god, received milk-based products as offerings. This was one of the reasons why the future of the Moiras was assured in Bengal. Separately, the Moiras were also patronized by the Bengali zamindars, who prized symbols of refinement such as the sandesh, and whose opulent lifestyles sometimes meant eating themselves to a standstill.

If it wasn't for the Moira community's ingenuity and creativity, we wouldn't have the mind-boggling variety of sandesh we see today in the sweetshops established by men such as Girish Chandra Dey and Nakur Chandra Nandy, a father-and son-in-law partnership which is said to have been created as early as 1844. As Krondl says, if there was one food that could represent the Bengal Renaissance, it was 'the urban, artisanal sweet'—the sandesh—made by confectioners in neighbourhood sweetshops.

Interestingly, while Bengal was on a sugar high, one of India's earliest thinkers and reformers was not taken in by this growing fascination with all things sweet. Swami Vivekananda was so put off by the culinary extravagances on display that he referred to the sweetshop as 'death's door'. Vivekananda's guru, Ramakrishna Paramhans, however, did not share his views, and was one of the biggest patrons of old Calcutta's Moira community. His favourite sweetshop was Bhim Chandra Nag. The shop also counted among its patrons the renowned mathematician and academic Ashutosh Mukherjee. The eponymous Nag, in fact, christened a variety of sandesh after him: ashubhog. Additionally, in order to show the city and the ruling elite's appreciation for a particularly liberal viceroy, a sandesh was named after Lord Ripon, the viceroy of India from 1880 to 1884. As recently as 1960, a sandesh called Bulganiner Bishmoy, or the wonder of Bulganin, was created for the Soviet premier who visited Bengal. A barrister—thankfully not one from my family—famously ordered sandesh in the shape of the gothic Calcutta High Court for his wedding.

While Bowbazar's Bhim Chandra Nag, established in 1826 by Paran Chandra Nag for his son, is considered the last word in sandesh, not every shop sells the same kind. And though there are many flavours of sandesh nowadays—many of which would make traditionalists baulk—from chocolate to salted caramel to mango sandesh, there are two traditional versions. White sandesh is made from chhana and sugar, and the light brown one with a caramel flavour is made with nolen gur, a kind of date palm jaggery. In fact, in my paternal family's village, the Guptipara makha sandesh, which is sold in terracotta urns covered with woven sal leaves, is a great delicacy. It is the simplest way of cooking sandesh since it doesn't require one to set the sandesh in moulds.

Today, sandesh is still loved for its unique taste by Bengalis and non-Bengalis alike. A morsel of this crumbly dessert flavoured with gur wins over the hearts of every person with a sweet tooth.

SANDESH

SERVES: 10   PREPARATION TIME: 2 HOURS

INGREDIENTS

Milk	1 litre
Lemon juice	1–1.5 tbsp
Palm jaggery	2 tbsp
or Sugar	3 tbsp

METHOD

Making chhana or cottage cheese

The main factor to get right here is the chhana or cottage cheese. Don't take a shortcut and use store-bought cottage cheese. Boil the milk. As the milk starts boiling, lower the flame. Add the lemon juice, or vinegar, and stir. The milk will curdle. Immediately take the pan off the flame.

Place a piece of muslin or a thin cotton napkin on a deep bowl. Empty the contents into the bowl lined with the muslin cloth. Tie the muslin and squeeze the whey, draining most of the water in the process.

Rinse the chhana in the muslin under a tap. This will remove the sourness of the lemon juice or vinegar from the paneer. Place a heavy bowl on the muslin-wrapped whey for 25–30 minutes.

Remove the paneer from the muslin sack and place in a plate or a tray. Knead the paneer with your hands till the mixture becomes smooth and less grainy. Add jaggery or sugar and knead for 2–3 minutes again. Once the jaggery/sugar has melted, it will release a little moisture into the mixture.

Heat a slightly deep pan. Put the paneer mixture in the pan on a low flame and keep stirring for about 10 minutes. The paneer will start drying and soon come together. Do not let it dry out too much, it should have a spongy texture. Remove from the pan and let the mixture cool.

Knead the mixture again to get a smooth consistency. Shape into round flat balls. You can make an indentation with your thumb and place a dry fruit of your choice in the centre. Ideally refrigerate for an hour before serving as this helps firm up the sandesh pieces.

Rosogolla
Who Stole My Cheese?

Few sweets are as contentious as the rosogolla—known outside of Bengal as rasgulla. 'Ros' means juice and 'golla' means ball. The rosogolla, which originated in East India—I'm not specifying whether in the state of Bengal or Odisha, as that's up for debate—is one of the few sweets you'll see all over the world. These slightly chewy and extremely soft cottage cheese or chhana balls soaked in sugar syrup are now sold in cans and carried to foreign shores by nostalgic Indians and tourists alike.

The rosogolla is created by using chhana, or curdled milk solids, to form roundels the size of golf balls. These white balls are then cooked and soaked in an extremely sugary, but light, syrup which is flavoured with cardamom or kevra (screwpine) or both. Rosogolla can be served piping hot or cold. Just like sandesh, rosogolla is an extremely inexpensive and popular sweet in Bengal, and distinctly local and authentic. It's also a multi-purpose sweet if you believe urban myths. It is claimed that if one has an upset stomach, they should squeeze the liquid from the rosogolla straight into their mouth—followed by the actual rosogolla, of course—as the healthy bacteria in the sweet syrup can battle any stomach infection. I wouldn't bank on this as a remedy, but it's an entertaining tale. The Odia version of the rosogolla is bigger and redder in colour than the Bengali one and, according to the people of Odisha, softer and less chewy. Nowadays, you even get baked variety rosogolla covered in kheer and baked till slightly caramelized. There's the nolen gur variety as well, which is a seasonal favourite.

You'd think that this sweet, which is loved in so many Indian states and has been exported to so many other countries, would act as a binding force in the country of its origin. Think again. West Bengal, which takes its sweets—and therefore its contribution to the national glycemic index—very seriously, has long claimed that it is the birthplace of the rosogolla. The gentleman who is supposed to have created it in the nineteenth century, Bengali confectioner Nobin Chandra Das, has a statue erected in his honour, and enjoys a stature similar to Columbus. Odisha though, begs to differ—so much so that it applied for a Geographical Index (GI) certificate for the dish. A GI status identifies a product as originating from a certain location, apart from guaranteeing its authenticity and distinctiveness. Odisha claims that the rosogolla was created within its borders as an offering called the khiramohana to Lord Jagannath.

The million-dollar question then remains: who invented the rosogolla?

The use of chhana seems to indicate that the rosogolla originated in Bengal as the practice of curdling milk was considered inauspicious and sacrilegious all over the country except in Bengal. Which is why only Bengal offers a surfeit of cottage cheese or chhana-based sweets. It is believed that chhana was created by the Portuguese in Bandel, their settlement in Bengal in the seventeenth century, when milk was curdled using acid. Bandel cheese, which was used to prepare rosogolla, is still very popular in Calcutta. Before the use of chhana, khoya—milk which has been reduced to almost a fifth of its original volume by slowly heating it—was used to prepare sweets. Sugar syrup, a key component of rosogolla, was also easy to prepare as fine grade sugar was in abundant supply in Calcutta in the mid-nineteenth century because of the sugar factories close to the city.

In Calcutta, Dhiman Das, a direct descendant of Nobin Chandra Das, has often said that the sweet was created by his ancestors. According to Das, Nobin Chandra Das opened his first sweetshop in Jorasanko in 1864. After this shop shut down, he opened another in Baghbazar in 1866, which is where he invented the rosogolla. According to various news reports, Nobin Chandra Das began experimenting with a new recipe in 1868 which required him to boil balls of chhana in sugar syrup.

But the balls kept falling apart until he added a secret enzyme to the chhana, which stopped the balls from disintegrating. Realizing that the more popular the sweet became, the more people would want to buy it, Nobin Chandra taught the art to other sweetshop owners. Dhimas Das is currently the executive director of KC Das Pvt Ltd, which began exporting rosogollas to other parts of the world in 1930.[*]

Another story claims that Haradhan Moira, a famous sweet maker who worked with the Pal Chowdhurys of Ranaghat, invented the rosogolla by accident when he dropped some chhana and semolina balls into a bubbling syrup.[†] In the late nineteenth and early twentieth centuries, two other sweet makers—the Mullicks of Bhowanipore who ran the famous Balaram sweetshop and Chittaranjan Mistana Bhandar of Sovabazar—refined the recipe further. There isn't much difference between the varieties of rosogollas available in Bengal, although some are made from jaggery now and have a more robust and earthy flavour, while others differ in how sweet the rosogolla and the syrup is.

What is referred to as rasbhari, rajbhog, and rasamalai in different parts of India are all versions of the rosogolla, which made its way beyond the borders of Bengal, thanks to a wealthy timber merchant, Bhagwandas Bagla, who lived in Bengal and loved rosogolla. The story goes that one day Bagla stopped by

---
[*]Amita Ghose, 'The rosogolla's bittersweet beginning: How a Calcutta confectioner created the dessert', *Firstpost,* 19 November 2017.
[†]Vikram Doctor, 'As the debate continues on the origin of rossogulla, take a look at the origins of the syrup or ras', *Economic Times,* 08 December 2017.

Nobin Chandra Das' sweetshop with his grandson, who was very thirsty. When Bagla asked for a glass of water for the boy, the water was served along with a portion of rosogolla. His grandson liked the taste of the sweet so much that Bagla not only started eating and enjoying it himself, he also decided to spread the joy to other parts of the country. Because of his timber business, the rosogolla found its way to Uttar Pradesh, Rajasthan, and many other parts of the country.*

The popularity of chhana-based sweets took a hit when, in 1965, the Congress chief minister Prafulla Sen banned milk sweets to increase West Bengal's dairy output—an acute scarcity of milk had led to the ban on chhana-based sweets in Calcutta. The production of milk per capita had plummeted to less than three ounces in the state, compared to Punjab's seventeen ounces and neighbouring Bihar's four ounces. The ban crippled the sweet industry of Bengal and a large number of shops shut down. This was followed by riots and protests. Despite this debacle; legacy shops such as KC Das also realized that they had to expand to markets outside Calcutta which led to their first shop in Bangalore.†

After all this trouble, a protracted debate ensued over rosogolla's origins. Food historians and the government in Odisha claim that the state was centuries ahead of Bengal when it came to the creation of the 'rasagola'—the Odia 'rosogolla'.

---

*Bishwabijoy Mitra, 'Who invented the rasgulla', *Times of India*, 06 July 2015; also see Priyadree Dasgupta, 'Sticky Sweet Success', *Indian Express*, 29 October 2011.
†Vikram Doctor and Writankar Mukherjee, 'The Great Rosogolla Revolt: When a Bengal CM banned sweets', *Economic Times*, 25 July 2015.

When Odisha applied for the GI status for the rasagola in 2015, the state's science and technology minister Pradip Kumar Panigrahi claimed that there was conclusive evidence that the rasagola had originated in Puri approximately 600 years ago.

According to some historians in Odisha, the Pahala rasagola was conceived in Puri as khiramohana and the goddess Lakshmi at the Jagannath Temple has been offered rasagola as bhog since the inception of the Jagannath Ratha Yatra. According to legend, Lord Jagannath, the goddess's consort, departed for a nine-day sojourn to his aunt's house accompanied by his brother Balabhadra and sister Subhadra without informing Lakshmi. When Jagannath returned from the Gundicha Yatra to the main temple in Puri, Lakshmi locked the Jai Vijay Dwar to prevent him and his retinue from entering the temple. To placate her, Jagannath offered rasagola to Lakshmi. The celebration of Jagannath's arrival after a nine-day ratha yatra is known as Niladri Bije. The ritual is completed with bachanika songs which symbolize the divine tussle between the two deities. The end of the divine spat is marked by the offering of the rasagola to appease the goddess Lakshmi. The ritual is still practised during the Puri Ratha Yatra festival and the holy chhappan bhog to Lord Jagannath originally included the rasagola. A few historians, including K. T. Achaya, have argued that the rasagola couldn't have been in the chhappan bhog, as it is made from curdled milk which, as we've seen, is considered inauspicious.

Another folk tale claims that there was an abundance of milk in a small village called Pahala, which is located between

Bhubaneswar and Cuttack. Since the excess milk was going to waste, a priest at the Jagannath Temple taught the villagers how to curdle milk and make rasagolas. This new dessert came to Bengal with the Odia cooks who were employed in Bengali homes from the mid-eighteenth century onwards.

The Odisha government, citing the tale of the Pahala rasagola, applied for GI status for the rasagola made in Pahala. What this meant is that if Odisha did get the approval from the Geographical Indication Registry of the Indian government, only sweet makers in the state would be able to call their product the Pahala rasagola. However, the Odisha government admitted that a committee set up to validate the claim found little written evidence to support the theory that rasagola was first created in Odisha. Since then, the Odia cultural scholar Asit Mohanty has found mention of the word 'rasagola' in the fifteenth-century Odia Dandi Ramayana—also known as Jagmohana Ramayana—written by the medieval poet Balaram Das. He has also quoted many other Odia and Sanskrit texts to prove that chhana was prepared in India long before the Portuguese arrived.

As this debate raged on, West Bengal received a GI tag for Banglar Rosogolla on 14 November 2017, which is now known as Rosogolla Day, following which festivities broke out across Calcutta. In Sovabazar, the statue of Nobin Chandra Das was garlanded and free rosogollas were distributed to people. In a strange twist to the cultural war between the two states, in 2019, Odisha was also granted a GI for the Odisha Rasagola, taking us nowhere nearer the end of this dispute. Two GI tags for the same sweet, however, mean that the regulatory authority recognizes that there can be two distinct varieties of rosogolla when it comes to taste and texture. But whatever the cultural wars across state borders, true lovers of the rosogolla couldn't give a damn because if anything bonds the country together, it is a tasty sweetmeat.

Since then, a tenuous peace has prevailed and dessert diplomacy has so far proved effective. Until, of course, someone finds the next sweet with contested origins.

ROSOGOLLA

SERVES: 24　　　　　　　　　　PREPARATION TIME: 1 HOUR

To be honest, I've never tried to make rosogollas. But since I was writing this book during the lockdown, I was stuck working from home and had more than ample time to make all the dishes I had never tried before. This is by far one of the easiest sweets to make, the trick is in the paneer or chhana. So just follow the chhana recipe from before (page 15) and you're set.

INGREDIENTS

Sugar	500 gms
Water	2 cups
Chhana or Paneer	250 gms

METHOD

Heat a pan on medium flame, add sugar and water, and stir till the sugar dissolves.

Knead the chhana, or paneer, till it softens and shape into balls. Ideally keep them small enough to fit into your palms as chhana expands while cooking. Bring the sugar syrup to a boil in a pressure cooker. Place the cottage cheese spheres in the pressure cooker, cover and cook under pressure for 5 minutes. Remove from heat immediately.

You can serve these cold or at room temperature. If you add grated jaggery to the sugar syrup, you'll get lovely light-brown rosogollas. But I'd try this with plain sugar before getting too adventurous.

The Christmas Cake
Culture Chameleon

Few cities in India—I'd go out on a limb here and actually say, no city in India—celebrates Christmas with as much fervour and enthusiasm as Calcutta does. So much so, it's the one city where you get Christmas cake through the year. The one dessert that symbolizes everything that John Lennon wanted us to aspire to. Imagine this—it's a city where a Jewish bakery is so well-known for its Christmas cakes that people carry these cakes back with them to other parts of the country or even outside India. It's where a Muslim baker makes Christmas cakes to order for Hindu clients, where the concept of celebrating Jesus Christ's birthday by having a slice or a pound of rum-soaked fruit cake seems as normal as wearing a monkey cap in December.

The reason why Christmas cake is one of the most intrinsic parts of the city's social fabric is because of the large Anglo-Indian population in the city and the state. As Minakshie Das Gupta, Bunny Gupta, and Jaya Chaliha have written in *The Calcutta Cookbook*, 'Christmas cake with Anglo-Indians and Goans is a matter of personal pride.... The ingredients: karamcha—the Calcutta cherry, a sour fruit, preserved and coloured a brilliant red—manufactured by the Kabuli dried-fruit sellers in the New Market; petha, crystallized white pumpkin, another ingredient is now added liberally as it is the cheapest of the preserved fruits; green cardamoms are added to cinnamon and finally a generous measure of rum poured into the mix.'* Baked in half pound bread tins, the cakes are exchanged between family and friends.

While I have never had one of these cakes baked by a local baker, in high school and college, I remember that my Anglo-Indian friends parents used to prepare their own Christmas cakes and wine, the cakes baked with marinated dried fruits which were soaked in rum the previous year. We'd go over, and it was a treat because we weren't given even a glass of wine to drink at home when we were eighteen or nineteen, and there we'd be served a slice of this rich fruit cake with a small glass of sweet fortified wine prepared from a home recipe passed down through the generations.

Burra Din or Christmas is an extremely important celebration in Calcutta. Children come home to visit their

---

*Minakshie Dasgupta, Bunny Gupta, Jaya Chaliha, *The Calcutta Cookbook: A Treasury of Over 200 Recipes from Pavement to Palace*, New Delhi: Penguin Books India, 1995.

families at this time, there's a general air of merriment, and for once Calcutta isn't hot and sweltering—although looking at the tweeds and deer hats on display, you'd think it snows in Calcutta.

But what makes the story of Christmas cake in Calcutta so much more important, especially in today's India where politicians make it a point to state caste-community-rank of anyone they share a meal with, is that in Calcutta, Christmas does not belong to any one religious group. The preparation of Christmas cake itself is a celebration of community, cutting across caste and religion.

One of the most famous Christmas cakes found in Calcutta is at the Jewish bakery in New Market, Nahoum's and Sons. Imagine that—a Jewish bakery helping celebrate the birthday of Jesus Christ! Nahoum's and Sons, which was founded by the Baghdadi Jew Israel Mordecai in 1902, is one of the last Jewish cultural institutions in the city.* I have been going there since I was five or six years old and have never seen the shop empty or seen anyone's orders getting mixed up. This is not a fancy patisserie. This is a non-air-conditioned store with glass windows which double up as shelves for the baked goods. So when you're staring in, you can look at the pizza puffs, cheese puffs, freshly baked bread, cheese straws, buttered garlic bread, mountains of plum cake, and 'rich' plum cake wrapped in butter paper—choose what you want. Nahoum's doesn't make Christmas cake through the year and you might not even manage to get your hands on a cake if you go to Nahoum's

---

*'Nahoum and Sons: Calcutta, India', *Atlas Obscura*, 30 December 2019.

too late in the week before Burra Din. Which is why we can assume that most people spend their twelve days of Christmas in Calcutta in a snaking queue of almost forty to fifty people, waiting patiently for their turn to make it to the store counter, and hoping that the bakery hasn't run out out of cake before they get a chance to lay their hands on it.

The cake itself is rich and dense, and you can taste the alcohol in every bite. It is so steeped in rum or brandy, that the cake—and pretty much any well-made Christmas cake—will taste as good as the day it was baked, even weeks later without being refrigerated and after a year in the fridge.

But not everyone can afford the cake at Nahoum's or trudge to New Market just to buy cake. In Taltala in Calcutta, marked by its narrow lanes, you'll find a slew of small hole-in-the-wall bakeries. It's a primarily Muslim locality and Kanchan Bakery, one of the most famous shops, even has a picture of Mecca on one of its walls. But the walls of this bakery are more syncretic than entire towns and cities in India today. Every December the bakery puts up a banner wishing everyone a Merry Christmas and asking people to reserve their baking slots from the first of December—one of the old-world charms of the bakeries in Taltala Lane. Cakes start being baked at Kanchan Bakery from the fifteenth of December, and this has not changed in the one and a half decades since I came to know of the bakery. Kanchan Bakery's existence can be traced back to around 65 years.

You don't get ready-made cakes at most of these bakeries. Instead the bakeries rent out their ovens by the hour. People go there with their pre-measured ingredients and if they haven't already mixed the batter, the bakers help them mix the ingredients into a batter, after which the helpful bakers pop the cake into the oven. The cakes in the bakeries that dot Taltala Lane are not baked in electric or gas ovens. The ovens are old wood-fired ones. And there is no one recipe. The bakers at Kanchan Bakery, or Dalia Bakery, or any of the others which rent out their ovens, will bake the cake according to the customer's preference and their recipe. It really doesn't get better than this.

This bespoke style of baking Christmas cakes is not new or seasonal for the Muslim bakeries. They also bake biscuits and breads using their own recipes and for people who bring in ingredients all year round.

If you'd rather buy your cake ready-made though, there's also the ninety-year-old Saldanha Bakery, which is known for a rendition of the Christmas cake with icing. At this Goan bakery, Debra Alexander uses the same recipe as her grandmother Ubeline Saldanha, who started this bakery with her husband, Ignatious, in the 1930s. The cakes at this bakery are the real deal with dried fruits and a rich denseness which is difficult to replicate unless the dried fruits have been marinating for months. Again, their customers aren't just Christians, but the largely non-Christian community in Calcutta that loves both cake and Burra Din in equal measure. Saldanha sells almost 600,000 pounds of cake through the Christmas season and almost all of it is made to order.

Cosmopolitan bakery chains like Monginis set up counters

outside their outlets to manage the rush for their 'rich plum cake', and Bengali ones such as Flury's and Kathleen's are known for marinating dried fruits and nuts in November. The Christmas cake in Calcutta, and elsewhere in India, is always dark in colour because of the use of brown sugar or unrefined sugar as an ingredient.

Then there's the seventy-year-old bakery founded by J. N. Barua, located in the primarily Anglo-Indian locality of Bow Barracks. These unassuming but warm bakeries that dot the city are known for their delicious wares, reliable recipes, and their trusted baking procedures.

The reason I've focused on Christmas cake in Calcutta as opposed to Goa or Pondicherry and other cities is because the people consuming these cakes in Calcutta aren't from just the Christian community. And also where else would you find so many bakeries run by people not belonging to the Christian faith and yet serving rum-soaked cakes at such a large scale for a festival which has little to do with them?

So who brought the first Christmas cake recipe to Calcutta? There are a couple of theories. One, of course, is common sense—there is some British influence given that Calcutta had such a large British community and that the cake recipe is very close to what you would find anywhere in Europe. The other is that it came to Calcutta via the Portuguese.

According to Purba Chatterjee, who is studying the Portuguese influence on food in India, 'Refined sugar came much later so the Portuguese introduced raw cane sugar in baking. Unlike the English, whose fruit cakes contained cherries and berries (dried cherries, currants, apricots, figs, raisins, and citrus peel, if you consult old cookbooks), the Portuguese adapted their recipes to what was available locally. Hence the addition of candied white pumpkin (murabba) and Bengal currant (koromcha or karaunda).'* This is a highly probable theory, given that the Portuguese were master confectioners.

But the first Christmas cake to be made in India, according to multiple reports, has been traced back to the Mambally family in Thiruvananthapuram known for baking the first Christmas cake in India nearly 140 years ago. According to Premnath Mambally, 'Those were days when the British ruled the Malabar region, which then came under the Madras Presidency. Bapu had started his "Mambally's Royal Biscuit Factory" in Thalassery in 1880, after going to Burma to learn the making of biscuits, bread, and buns. He began with 140 varieties of biscuits. Three years later, Mr (Murdoch) Brown, who owned one of the estates nearby, brought a cake to Bapu and told him all he knew about how to bake one—the ingredients included a French Brandy. Bapu took it as a challenge but made the cake with the local brew. When the Britishman tasted the cake, he famously said "excellent" and ordered twelve more. The date was December 20, 1883.'† Today however, Santha Bakery, which is run by Mambally Bapu's descendants, is known for its

---
*Paromita Sen, 'How sweet, Portuguese', *The Telegraph*, 17 October 2021.
†Cris, 'How Mambally Bapu baked the first Christmas cake in Kerala in 1883', *News Minute*, 24 December 2021.

The Christmas Cake

biscuits more than it is for its Christmas cakes.

Many regions and towns have their own unique version of the Christmas cake which is prepared and sold only during Christmas. The Pondicherry Christmas cake has Creole roots. It's a rich, alcohol-soaked cake (either rum or brandy) and is prepared with roasted semolina and ghee, marinated cashews and raisins, candied fruits, and citrus peels. This is another one of those cakes that can be kept in an airtight tin for months on end.

The Anglo-Indian railway colony of Allahabad might have influenced the spiced, rum-soaked Allahabadi Christmas cake. This cake is known for its distinctive use of petha, or ash gourd candy, and marmalade, and uses ghee instead of butter and is flavoured with a mix of nutmeg, cinnamon, fennel, mace, and ginger.

While we might rage against the colonizers for looting us, and I understand that it's far from the fairest exchange, a little credit must be given to them for introducing the Christmas cake or even cake to our shores. The dessert that ensures that all communities come together for the joy of partaking in the perfect Christmas cake.

Payasam, Payesh, Kheer
The Three Avatars of Sweet Pudding

If there's one dessert that seems to connect all of India, from north to south and east to west, it would be the rice pudding. This dessert even binds Hindu and Muslim homes together and hardly ever will an auspicious event, such as a puja or an Eid, not have some form of rice pudding. Call it kheer, payasam, payesh, or phirni, most communities and regions seem to have a version of a slow-cooked rice pudding sweetened with jaggery or sugar, with or without dried fruit, and sometimes with fresh fruit. A bowl of this dessert is a simple and low-cost, but extremely luscious, dessert served at home.

Kheer is often made with rice, but there is no hard and fast rule to this, which is why one community's kheer preparation could well be another community's payasam or payesh.

Every traditional celebration I have been to in India—Hindu, Muslim, or Parsi—has always had a serving of kheer or payasam served at the end of the meal or as a religious offering. In Bengal though, kheer does not have rice in it. But that might just be Bengal acting contrarian because kheer, according to food historian K. T. Achaya's research, is indeed a 'sweet confection based on rice'.[*] The history of kheer and payasam is vast and very old, unlike most other desserts.

When kheer is prepared for rituals, the rice is first lightly fried in ghee, before simmering in sugared milk. A kheer of jowar, or sorghum, is mentioned in the fourteenth-century *Padmavat* of Gujarat. Other cereals such as barley can be used as well, and sometimes no cereal is added. Payasam can be thought of as a thinner version of kheer, although this doesn't hold true across all regions of India.

Payasam or khirika first finds mention in Buddhist-Jain canonical literature around 400 BCE. The Mahabharata also describes an episode where Yudhishthira feeds a thousand Brahmins a feast that includes cooked preparations of rice and milk mixed with ghee and honey.[†] In the fourteenth century, the Moroccan scholar and explorer Ibn Battuta documented how grains and millets were cooked in buffalo milk. A feast for

---

[*] K. T. Achaya, *Indian Food: A Historical Companion*, New Delhi: Oxford University Press, 1994.
[†] S. R. Barela and R. R. Shelke, 'Studies on Acceptability, Chemical Composition and Cost Structure of Kheer Prepared from Cow Milk Blended with Coconut Milk', *International Journal of Current Microbiology and Applied Sciences*, Volume 6, Number 11, 2017, pp. 2527-32.

King Shrenika, described in the *Bhavissayatakaha* from 1000 CE, lists as the last item served—one 'half-boiled milk' containing sugar, honey, and saffron, which sounds very close to kheer.

What is interesting is that the description and preparation of payasam seems unchanged in its current form since it was first mentioned. A payasam made with vermicelli can be found in a work in Kannada from 1222 CE. Achaya refers to a 'bead-like payasam' made from sago perhaps, in a work from 1235 CE. *Manasollasa*, the earliest known 'non-medical' text on Indian food, describes a dish of clotted cream flakes in sugar and milk called 'kene payasa' too.

Coming to its fraternal twin, kheer, the name is derived from the Sanskrit word ksheer for milk, and the same kshirika that refers to any dish prepared with milk.

In Bengal, Muslim cooking influences were first seen in the kitchens of the upper classes and the nawabs who represented the Mughal empire in Bengal. This led to a uniquely Bengali–Muslim cuisine which is different from other Muslim culinary traditions in India such as the Mughlai, Awadhi, and Nizami cuisines. Bengali–Muslim food, and therefore even the phirni in this cuisine, is less rich and the phirni in this cuisine uses yoghurt and lime instead of the cream present in the phirni of other Muslim cultures across India.

Kheer in Bengal refers to thickened milk, which is reduced to half its quantity over a low flame, sweetened with sugar, and served as dessert after dinner. It is not very different from payasam, save for the absence of rice. During Janmashthomi, which marks the birth of the Hindu god Krishna, a special kheer is prepared to break the fasting period that many devout Hindus observe. The ripe palm or taal is cooked with milk and grated coconut to prepare a creamy kheer which is an East Bengal specialty. Another popular version of kheer is the kamala kheer, or orange kheer, which requires quite a bit of expertise to prepare. It is almost always served during Durga Puja—the festival to celebrate the return of goddess Durga to her parental home. On Ashthami, the eighth day of the festival, milk is cooked till it reduces to half its quantity, after which sugar is added to the thickened milk. Then, tangerines from the first crop are peeled and the inner pulp is added to the kheer after it has cooled down. This is considered a delicacy as tangerines tend to be very expensive, and moreover, the process of peeling them is tedious, and if added before the kheer has cooled down to the right temperature, it can curdle the milk and ruin all the hard work that has gone into it. As if in a bid to prove its worth against the tediousness of the process, it's a beautifully aromatic and delicious dessert.

In Bengal, payesh is made in honour of the goddess Lakshmi during Lakshmi Puja. Traditionally, payesh is always cooked outside the kitchen in sanctified surroundings, in a special utensil and on a portable stove. Earlier this stove would use coal as the heating agent. While there are many kinds of payesh now that don't use rice, the dessert still relies heavily on milk. You will never see the use of cream or condensed milk, as these were unheard of in Bengal and would never have survived without refrigeration in the humid climes there. Milk is thickened by slowly cooking it over moderate heat and stirring in sugar continually, other than in the winter, when date palm or khejur gur is added to imbue the payesh with a lovely brown colour. Once the milk has thickened after almost an hour, rice fried in ghee is added to the pot—usually gobindobhog or any other small-grained variety of rice. When the rice is cooked— take care that it doesn't turn glutinous—sugar is added to the simmering kheer. The kheer is usually topped off with soaked, lightly fried or dried fruits and nuts. Some preparations add cardamom and others raisins. The result is a creamy, sweet, but not cloyingly rich, rice dessert.

That kheer and payesh are loved across the country is a widely known fact, one which is visible in the innumerable regional preparations of this dessert. The lesser known Sheherwali cuisine of the Jain Oswal community in Murshidabad, which settled in Bengal 300 years ago, is a mix of vegetarian Rajasthani flavours blended with Bengali spices such as paanch phoron and nawabi ingredients such as saffron, rose water, and dry fruits. This Sheherwali cuisine has an interesting version of kheer—a kachha aam ka kheer prepared with green mango.

More than kheer, payasam is extremely popular in southern India. It is served both at home and during celebrations and occasions. And southern India, with its centuries-old tradition of documenting food, gives us a detailed history of the long relationship the region has with this preparation. According to Achaya in *A Historical Dictionary of Indian Food*, 'kollu', or horse gram was used to prepare a sweet payasam served during funerals.

Payasam's centuries-old connection with India can be found in the *Supa Shastra*, a book on food, written by the Chengalva king Mangarasa III in 1516 CE. From the Chengalva dynasty, that was subordinate to Hoysala kings in sixteenth-century Karnataka, Mangarasa was known to be a talented and experimental chef. *Supa Shastra* is his treatise in Sanskrit and loosely means 'the science of cooking'. Mangarasa could be considered one of India's earliest food historians given that he did not limit himself simply to the art of cooking, but also focused on tracing the origins of food recipes. Chamarasa, a fifteenth-century Virashaiva poet in the Kannada language, also refers to payasam in a 1430 CE text.

The vast variety of payasams don't seem to have altered much over time—sweet boiled rice payasam in milk (of which paramanna seems to have been the most intricately flavoured), a rice-derived vermicelli payasam, and a mixed rice-wheat payasam are mentioned then and still exist today. Milk is mentioned as the main ingredient for payasam. There is a mention of semiya payasam, described as 'the eye of the moon', and also payasams of wheat, vermicelli, and chana or chickpeas. A wedding feast of the Nairs, a martial caste from Kerala, serves payasams made of milk, coconut milk, rice, pulses, and bananas.

In fact, seviyan, a thicker and shorter form of vermicelli made from hard wheat, is used to make payasam in South India even today. Muslim households use a very thin version of the seviyan on Eid.

Interestingly, the prathaman or traditional payasam of Kerala uses rice, milk, and coconut milk, along with dry fruits or pulses. Some varities of the payasam also use paper-thin shreds of a rice roll, which are cooked separately and added to the sweetened milk later. In northern Karnataka, one of the unique dishes served at Lingayat weddings is soute bija huggi, or broken wheat kheer, named so because it resembles tiny soute bija or cucumber seeds.

A very unique version of kheer can be found in the Northeast. The chakhau anuba kheer is a black rice pudding from Manipur made from the locally grown black rice grains that are popular in the neighbouring states as well. Black rice is also referred to as 'forbidden rice' in Manipur and turns a deep purple shade when cooked. This rice has immense nutritional and health benefits, it is rich in antioxidants, and is a natural detoxifier. Even more importantly, from a culinary viewpoint, black rice has a very interesting flavour and is nutty in taste and texture. Although the rice takes longer to cook—it takes almost twenty-four hours to prepare the kheer—it is well worth the purple richness which emerges at the end.

There is a foreign influence to kheer as we know it, though. The Persians, who introduced phirni in India, were the first ones to introduce the use of rose water and dry fruits in kheer—an influence that has prevailed. The shola, a rice pudding specialty from Iran and Afghanistan, which can be both savoury and sweet, is made with saffron and rose water and is another variation of kheer. The shola is a lot like the Afghani sheer brinji, which saw the introduction of expensive ingredients such as kevra essence, dried fruit, and edible gold leaf. It is only after sheer brinji was created and became popular that kheer, which till then was served as a hot dessert, began to be served cold.

That kheer and payasam and thickened milk puddings have been commonplace in India for centuries might explain the popularity of these preparations across the country. Should you always know whether you're having a spoonful of kheer or payasam or payesh when served a rice pudding or a thickened milk pudding? Why bother? A payasam or payesh or kheer by any other name is just as sweet, give or take a few grains of rice.

KHEER

SERVES: 8   PREPARATION TIME: 1 HOUR

INGREDIENTS

Rice	4 tbsp
Milk	1 litre, full cream
Sugar	200 gms
Dry fruits	A handful
Cardamom	1 tsp, crushed
Saffron	8 to 10 strands, soaked in milk

METHOD

Soak the rice in water for 20–30 minutes. Boil milk in a thick pan over low heat till it reduces by half. Add the rice and bring to a boil for a minute or so.

Reduce the heat and let the milk and rice simmer for almost 30 minutes. The mixture will have a soft pish-pash or khichdi consistency.

Add dry fruits, cardamom, saffron, and sugar, and mix. Remove from heat and serve warm or at room temperature.

Halwa
The Arab Who Strayed onto the Indian Palate

The first—and possibly only—Indian dessert my mother cooked for my father when they settled into their home in Delhi, as a young couple with two toddlers, was gajar ka halwa. Gajar ka halwa is a slow-cooked north Indian dessert of grated carrots, simmered in milk, ghee, and a generous portion of refined sugar. The end product, which you will find in many north Indian homes, is an orange-hued, textured, and sweet dessert. It's a different matter that my mother cooked enough halwa to feed at least twenty hungry people. You can't really cook small quantities of gajar ka halwa, and since my father refused to eat any after the first serving, unsuspecting guests had to eat the halwa for weeks on end. But that's a story for another day.

Over a decade, I have realized that gajar ka halwa is one of the most popular desserts in north Indian homes, especially in Delhi where I live, across all sections of society. The three main ingredients are easy to find, not particularly expensive, and the halwa itself is a perfectly warm dessert for Delhi's frigid winters. Who would think that we have the Dutch to thank for this wonder! It's a tenuous connection, but orange carrots were created in the seventeenth century, when Dutch farmers decided to pay tribute to William of Orange. Carrots soon found their way to Punjab through Afghanistan and the rest, as they say, is history. Women cooked gajar ka halwa for hours on coal stoves, waiting for the grated carrot to cook through while the milk it was cooking in reduced to less than half its quantity. Of course, now people use khoya instead of milk to save time.

While I was scripting a food show on the unique foods of India, I discovered that the orange gajar ka halwa isn't the only variety available. There's a less common white version which is available at a century-old shop in Old Delhi called Sheeren Bhawan. Made from white carrots sourced from Ghaziabad, this version is available only between mid-December and mid-February. The grated white carrots do not shrink and are slightly less sweet—giving the halwa a slightly more nuanced look and taste.

Lucknow, the city of great food, serves another version, which is as tasty and, again, less sweet. The black carrot halwa, which hasn't been replicated in Delhi—although I have seen mountains of black carrots in the vegetable mandi—is a less grainy and earthier version which lends itself very well to the realm of desserts. The grated carrots are cooked with milk—no shortcuts involving khoya here—sugar, and ghee to create a deep purple dessert which would appeal to anyone who prefers less sugar and more flavour.

Halwas are extremely common in North India and sometimes in the South, but are cooked less frequently in East or West India. Although Bengal has a cholar dal halwa, I've only ever heard of it and never tasted it in all these decades. In *The Illustrated Foods of India*, food historian K. T. Achaya writes: 'In India, it [halwa] connotes softly firm desserts made from a range of materials: wheat flour, wheat grits, vermicelli, Bengal gram flour, fruits like banana and date, nuts like almond, and vegetables like pumpkins and dates.' But this definition doesn't include all the halwas you can find in India. Far removed from these, there are some non-vegetarian variants such as gosht halwa and ande ka halwa which are worth mentioning.

Giving a whole new meaning to the word 'sweet meat', the gosht halwa is a translucent, succulent dessert soaked in ghee and cooked with tender lamb mince. The recipe is referred to in old Persian recipe books, and khansamas who worked in Old Delhi homes have recreated the dish from memory, turning out a delightful dessert prepared by cooking meat for hours by stirring it with milk and sugar till it amalgamates into a thick halwa which is then flavoured with saffron and cardamom. This preparation is supposed to have originated in Rampur, Uttar Pradesh. Ande ka halwa, or egg halwa, is made by cracking eggs into a pan with ghee, milk, sugar, and dried fruits. The mixture is cooked until a thick custard forms, which is then sprinkled with saffron.

Most Indian halwas, however, use grains, such as the suji halwa and atta halwa. For example, in Gujarat, you get the mohanlal, a halwa made of besan or chickpea flour. Like many desserts, it is very common to serve halwa during celebrations or rituals. Kada prasad is a wheat halwa which the Sikh community serves at baptisms, marriages, and cremations. The jauzi halwa of Lucknow is made with almonds, milk, and saffron, and is supposed to help build immunity. In Karnataka, kesari bhat is prepared by cooking wheat semolina or suji in ghee, and then with saffron and sugar.

There's a quaint anecdote attached to the Sindhi community's Karachi halwa—a chewy halwa which looks more like a gelatinous fudge than halwa. Following the Partition, the nomenclature referring to the origins of the dessert suddenly became a bone of contention. Many renamed it Bombay halwa, primarily because Bombay and Karachi had flourished as twin port cities, and most migrants from Karachi settled in Bombay. In Delhi, however, the halwa kept being referred to as Karachi halwa and remains extremely popular as a gift because of its long shelf life. In fact, there's a bureaucratic tradition of the Indian finance minister preparing and offering halwa to their finance ministry colleagues before presenting the budget. Which might also explain the mish-mash we are usually served hot in the guise of the budget.

So where did halwa come to India from? The word 'halwa' comes from the Arabic word 'hulw', which means sweet, and 'when first used in English denoted a Turkish confection of ground sesame seeds and honey', according to Achaya. That the dish came to India via trade routes is underlined by the fact that two important port cities—Karachi and Kozhikode—have their own distinct version of the halwa.

The thirteenth-century Arabic text, *Kitab al-Tabikh*, written by Muḥammad ibn al-Ḥasan Ibn al-Karim, who had compiled a recipe book of Arabic dishes, is the first known text to mention halwa. The text mentions eight different varieties of halwa along with each of their recipes.

The *Ain-i-Akbari*, written in the sixteenth century by Akbar's court historian, Abul Fazl, mentions halwa as one of the dishes prepared for Akbar as part of the repertoire of dishes served during safiyana—the days during which Akbar abstained from meat. According to Edward Terry, Thomas Roe's chaplain, halwa was eaten by the poorer classes of Muslims at breakfast, along with naan, keema, sheer brinji, and dried fruits.

According to the quarterly *Repast*, and many food historians, including Rana Safvi, the origins of halwa have been repeatedly traced back to Arabia. Which might explain why mithai makers in India are referred to as 'halwais'. Safvi refers to *Guzishta Lucknow* by Abdul Halim Sharar, who lived in Lucknow in the late nineteenth and early twentieth centuries. 'In *Guzishta Lucknow*, Sharar writes that taking the name into consideration, halwa originated in Arabic lands and came to India via Persia.'* There is no certainty though, of the exact period when halwa entered Indian kitchens. The original Middle Eastern dessert was supposedly made from a paste of dates and milk.

The kitchens of Suleiman the Magnificent, who ruled the Ottoman Empire from 1520 to 1566, are said to have had a special sweets section called The Helvahane or The Dessert and Candy Room.

According to Chicago-based food historian Colleen Taylor Sen, the author of *Feasts and Fasts*, 'halwa arrived in India with the advent of the Delhi Sultanate, gaining popularity from the early thirteenth to the mid-sixteenth century.'† *Nimatnama*, a medieval cookbook written for the Sultan of Malwa in 1500, mentions the halwa and its recipe.

The theories are as many as the varieties of halwa found in India. Irrespective of its origins, it is fair to say that halwa is one of the most versatile of Indian desserts which seems to have found favour and flavour unique to each of the regions in which it can be found.

---

*Yashee, 'Explained: A sweet tale of how India imported halwa, and made it its own', *Indian Express*, 22 January 2020.
†Colleen Taylor Sen, *Feasts and Fasts: A History of Food in India*, London: Reaktion Books, 2014.

RAGI HALWA

SERVES: 4   PREPARATION TIME: 20 MINUTES

INGREDIENTS

Ragi flour	500 gms
Ghee	200 gms
Jaggery or brown sugar	300 gms
Cardamom powder	1 tsp, ground
Cashews	8 to 10, roasted

METHOD

Heat ghee in a pan. Add ragi flour and fry for about 5 minutes on medium heat while stirring constantly. In another pan, mix the jaggery/brown sugar with water and bring to a boil.

Pour the jaggery syrup into the flour, breaking all lumps, and cook for 5–10 minutes till the mixture thickens. Do not let it dry out too much. Remove from the pan and garnish with chopped cashews before serving.

Barfi
When Art Outdoes Nature

Very few sweets can boast a richer history than that of the barfi. While it gained pan-Indian popularity during the Independence movement, you can trace its origins to the Sikhs and ultimately the Persians. But no matter what its historical provenance, barfi continues to signify a morsel of slow-cooked sugary goodness.

At celebrations or community festivals, you can bet your last paisa that a barfi will make its way onto your plate or to your home, especially if you happen to live in the northern or western parts of India. Come Diwali, it's impossible to find a home doesn't have at least one box of kaju barfi sitting in the kitchen or on the dining table.

Barfi is made from condensed milk, ghee, and sugar. These

ingredients are cooked together into a paste, and then set, after which the paste is cut into diamond and square pieces, with varq, or an edible silver leaf, on top. Fudge-like in consistency and less sweet than most Indian sweets, there are many reasons why barfi is such a popular dessert.

One of the primary reasons for its popularity is that the barfi is very durable, unlike other temperamental Indian sweets. It can weather the heat of North India and the humidity of western India—this is a resilient sweet if ever there was one. It can remain in a cool place for months in an airtight container, without losing its texture or flavour, which makes it the best gift to present people with when you're travelling abroad or meeting them for a festival. Also like fudge, barfi is prepared and sold in a number of flavours, mostly fragrant, such as chocolate, rose water, cardamom, and pistachio, and sometimes even fruity ones like orange, mango, and strawberry. The kaju barfi—which is extremely popular and expensive—is made with ground cashews that give the barfi an ivory-like appearance. The pista barfi uses ground pistachios and can sometimes be a vibrant green. The primary ingredient in each barfi decides its appearance and the sugar acts as a binding force.

One of the most common questions asked in a school quiz revolves around the origins of the word 'barfi'. The sweet was supposedly named after the Persian and Urdu word baraf, which translates to snow, because when these diamond-shaped sweets are stacked together, they resemble the white peaks of snowy mountains. I've never found any written documentation of this.

Another story goes that kaju barfi was created under Mughal rule, during Jahagir's reign. There's a north Indian connection to this story—Jahagir had captured many Sikh gurus and kings and incarcerated them in the Gwalior fort. One of the prisoners was Guru Hargobind, the sixth Sikh guru, who spent his time teaching other prisoners and the guards. When Jahagir declared that the Guru would be released, he also, in a show of royal ingenuity and magnanimity, announced that anyone who could hold on to Guru Hargobind's robe while he walked out would be granted freedom as well. Legend has it that Guru Hargobind asked the other prisoners to create a robe long enough for everyone in the prison to hold on to.

And so all the prisoners held onto Guru Hargobind's robe and walked free. For Sikhs, this day is celebrated as Bandhi Chhor Diwas. As a show of appreciation for the Guru, Jahagir's royal chef prepared kaju barfi. The kaju barfi that was prepared was originally made with thickened milk or rabri, and mixed with ground cashews and almonds. Interestingly, almost all references to kaju katli, as kaju barfi is commonly called, show that it originated in western India. The most authentic version of this sweet can be found in cities like Mumbai, Ahmedabad, and Surat.

Another extremely popular but different variety of barfi is called the dhoda barfi, which originated in Pakistan as Khushabi dhoda. Dhodha barfi is of a rich, grainy texture and its origins can be traced back to Khushab, a city in Pakistan's Punjab province. It's one of those prized recipes which every shop in the region claims it has invented.*

The Persian connection can be found here as well. The word 'khushab' is a combination of two Persian words, 'khush' which means 'sweet', and 'aab' which is water—the name of the sweet deceptively refers to 'sweet water'. According to local folklore, Persian invaders from the west first used this word to describe the waters of the Jhelum, on the banks of which sat the historical city of Dhodha. The dhoda barfi was supposedly invented by a local wrestler named Pehlwan Hans Raj in Khushab in 1902. He wanted to create a snack to eat during his wrestling sessions—a snack that was dry, easy to cart around, and full of nutrients. There is no written proof of this, but it's an urban legend which is often repeated.

Since necessity is the mother of invention, the wrestler turned part-time chef experimented with different combinations of high energy ingredients such as wheat, milk, and dry fruits. And voila, he came up with the dhodha barfi. The recipe was supposedly created in 1912 and after Partition in 1947, when his family moved to Kotkapura in western Punjab, they introduced the recipe to the local sweet makers in Khushab.

The dhoda barfi can be bought in most parts of South Asia, packaged in air-tight boxes—but it can also be made at home. The ingredients are easily procured: milk, sugar, broken wheat, clarified butter, dry fruits such as pistachios, walnuts, cashews, and even peanuts. The broken wheat needs to be soaked in milk

---

*Owais Qarni, 'From royals to masses, few can resist Khushabi dhodha', *Express Tribune*, 03 February 2019.

till it absorbs and becomes grainy and thick. The broken wheat is then cooked with sugar till it sticks together. The brown colour of the dhoda barfi comes from the slow cooking and is an indicator of it being cooked through. After letting it cool down, it is transferred to a tray greased with clarified butter and flattened out. Slivered cashew nuts, pistachios, walnuts, and almonds are sprinkled on top. The barfi is then cut into squares. The broken wheat makes it very different from the kaju barfi or the usual barfis, which are far smoother in texture.

Another historical tale about the barfi is that of the tirangi barfi—or the tricolour barfi—of Benaras. During the freedom struggle, the British government would censor newspapers and posters weren't allowed to be plastered on walls. As a result, freedom fighters had to come up with new ways of sloganeering and spreading the call for independence. The tirangi barfi—which makes an appearance every Republic and Independence Day in sweetshops across North India—was created as one of the 'rashtriya sweets' by the local sweetshop Ram Bhandaar to represent the Swaraj flag, the predecessor to the Indian flag today, as a show of support to the freedom fighters and Gandhi. Since there were no artificial food colours at the time, a layer of barfi made from oranges was placed alongside khoya or coconut barfi, and pistachio flavoured barfi was used for the green stripe. The barfi was used to commemorate the unfurling of the flag on the banks of the Ravi by Jawaharlal Nehru.[*]

---

[*]Pushpesh Pant, '1947: A story of tricolour "halwas" and subversive "mithais"', *Livemint*, 11 August 2017.

The Independence movement and Partition led to a large number of culinary creations in India. Some to charm the British, some to celebrate victories, and other as remnants of a homeland left behind. So every time you bite into a barfi, in a way, you're biting into more than just slow-cooked broken wheat and sugar—it's really a walk through India's past.

KAJU BARFI

SERVES: 8   PREPARATION TIME: 30 MINUTES

INGREDIENTS

Cashews	1 cup, chopped
White sugar	½ cup
Water	¼ cup, room temperature
Cardamom powder	a pinch, freshly ground
Ghee	1 tsp

METHOD

Grind the cashews to a powder.

In a hot frying pan, pour sugar along with water and stir. Turn the flame to low and keep stirring till a sugar syrup forms. Add the ground cashews and mix well. Add cardamom powder and continue to mix till the mixture becomes doughy. Add ghee and stir till the ghee melts through the dough mixture. Take the pan off the stove.

Empty the mixture onto your counter or into a bowl, grease your hands with ghee, and knead until the dough is smooth. Form a ball with the dough and cover it with a slightly damp cloth. Take a baking tray, or a flat tray, and place a sheet of butter paper on it. Grease the butter paper with some ghee. Place the dough on the baking sheet and use a rolling pin to spread the dough flat. Keep the thickness to ¼ of an inch. Let this set in the fridge for an hour.

With a sharp knife, cut the dough into diamond shapes. Sprinkle some dried fruits or varq on it before serving.

Gulab Jamun
Everybody's Celebration Sweetmeat

One of my favourite memories from when I was a child of six or seven is attending my best friend's birthday party where, alongside all the food at lunch, there used to sit a large glass bowl of the softest gulab jamuns imaginable, floating in warm sugar syrup. Every year, I'd take one gulab jamun—or was it two—and cut into it with a spoon, to reveal its soft spongy filling soaked in sugar, and marvel at the fact that my friend's mother had made this from scratch. It had just the right amount of sweetness, was extremely soft to bite into, and always somewhat warm. To date, gulab jamuns remain my favourite Indian dessert.

These deep-fried balls made of milk powder, flour, butter, and milk are popular in India, Pakistan, Bangladesh, Nepal, and almost the entire subcontinent. The gulab jamun was even named the national dessert of Pakistan in 2019.

The gulab jamun is common, but exquisite, in the sense that you will find it on menus across India. I've even had gulab jamun served to me in Indian restaurants and at five-star hotel buffets across the world. The name, loosely translated, means rose-fruit, where 'gulab' refers to rose and 'jamun' refers to the slightly tart java plum which is found all over the subcontinent and which the sweet resembles in shape and colour. The 'gulab' could also be a nod to the sugar syrup which the gulab jamun is served in, which is often scented with rose water.

The addition of rose water hints at one possible origin of the gulab jamun. While there is no documented proof for this, many food historians claim that the gulab jamun could have been introduced by Central Asian invaders to the subcontinent. Others claim that the dessert was an accidental creation by Mughal emperor Shah Jahan's chef, but I haven't discovered any credible source for this claim. What I have discovered is that the dessert is quite similar to the Arabic sweet luqmat-al-qadi, which was introduced to India by the Mughal emperors.

The difference between the two sweets is that luqmat-al-qadi is less brown in colour and often soaked in honey as opposed to sugar syrup. The luqmat dates back to the thirteenth-century Abbasid caliphate, and is mentioned in several accounts of food at the time, including *Kitab al-Tabikh* where it is called luqam al-qadhi. The historian Muhammad bin Hasan al-Baghdadi mentions the sweet as early as the thirteenth century. A survey of antiquity also shows this to be one of the oldest recorded desserts in the world where, according to Greek poet Callimachus, these deep-fried balls were soaked in honey and served to the winners of the Olympic Games as 'honey tokens'.

It is interesting to note that the preparation of the luqmat is the same as that of the gulab jamun. A ball of dough is fried in oil and then dipped in flavoured syrup which—depending on the country we're in—could be made from orange juice, rose water, honey, or even lemon juice. The Iranian bamiyeh and the Turkish tulumba, both of which are similar to the gulab jamun, are made from unleavened dough that is fried and dipped in sugar syrup. Unlike the gulab jamun, the bamiyeh is eaten cold. The lokma, which can be found in Turkey, is very similar to the gulab jamun as we know it in India, and is served with coffee and coated with chocolate sauce or honey or sesame or grated walnuts. It's possible that Mughal cooks were inspired by the Persian and Turkic desserts, and added rose water to make this indulgent dessert cooling in South Asia's hot weather. Flavours such as khus and rose, which are considered to be cooling, have also entered India thanks to Turkish and Persian influences.

While some recipes use yoghurt in the dough, others use baking powder or milk powder, and some Pakistani recipes I came across even use egg. Saffron and cardamom are often used to make the sweet notes a little more complex. The appearance of the sweet varies from country to country and state to state within India. In his 1994 book, *Indian Food: A Historical Companion*, the food historian K.T. Achaya describes gulab jamun as, 'Balls of chenna or khoya or paneer, kneaded using maida and then deep-fried till they become dark brown on the surface, and then gently boiled in a medium-thick sugar syrup, sometimes flavoured with rose essence.' Some states make round dough balls, others make a doughnut-shaped version and in Bengal and North India, we even have oval-shaped gulab jamuns stuffed with a cardamom or clove.

After learning how the gulab jamun is prepared, I was even more impressed by the fact that my friend's mother was cooking it at home. It's a tedious process. First, khoya is made by constantly stirring milk over a low flame till it becomes solid. This milk solid is mixed with flour and kneaded into a dough, which is shaped into small balls and deep-fried. These fried balls are then dipped in sugar syrup which is usually flavoured with cardamom, rose water, or strands of saffron. The deep brownish-red colour of the gulab jamun is from the solid milk and sugar in the mixture, which caramelizes to give it this hue.

In Bengal, and especially in my hometown of Calcutta, you get a black variant of the gulab jamun which is called kalo jaam by Bengalis, or kala jamun others, and literally translates to black fruit. The dough balls of kalo jaam are coated with sugar before frying, which gives this variant its blackish colour. The other difference between the two is that gulab jamun is usually served hot or warm, but kalo jaam is usually served at room temperature. The kalo jaam also tends to be less soft than the gulab jamun because its outer layer is caramelized. Another variant of the gulab jamun in Bengal is the pantua, which is oval-shaped and similar to the langcha, which supposedly originated in Shaktigarh, in the Burdwan district of West Bengal.

But the most interesting of the variants according to me, because of its background story, is the ledikenni. The ledikenni was created for Lady Canning, the wife of Charles Canning, who was the governor-general of India from 1856 to 1862. The story goes that Lady Canning had asked the sweet maker Bhim Chandra Nag to create a sweet for her birthday—as one ought to for their birthday. Bhim Chandra Nag made a hybrid form of a langcha, which is a little bit of both pantua and gulab jamun. Another version of the story goes that the sweet was prepared to commemorate Lady Canning's visit to India. The sweet was referred to as ledikenni by the locals and is definitely worth trying. You shouldn't confuse it with the pantua though, which is more oval in shape than the ledikeni. The ledikenni, which was created at the behest of the erstwhile vicereine, is oblong and infused with cardamom essence and a raisin at its centre.

Persian, Turkish, Greek…whatever its antecedents, I'd strongly recommend ordering a bowl of gulab jamun, pantua, kalo jam, or ledikenni to complete your meal. I've rarely tasted a sweet made of such simple ingredients that is so gratifying. It's soaked not just in the goodness of sugar syrup, but in centuries of historical tradition.

GULAB JAMUN

SERVES: 20 PORTIONS PREPARATION TIME: 1 HOUR

Like many Indian sweets, this isn't for the calorie conscious at all. It's deep-fried but delightful to taste. Nothing beats a warm gulab jamun.

INGREDIENTS

FOR THE GULAB JAMUN

Khoya	200 gms khoya
All-purpose flour	3 tbsp
Baking soda	¼ tsp
Ghee	1 tbsp
Milk	To knead
Dry fruits	To garnish

FOR THE SUGAR SYRUP

Sugar	2 cups
Water	2 cups
Cardamom powder	1 tsp, freshly ground

METHOD

In a large bowl, mix the khoya with the flour, baking soda, and ghee. Knead the mixture and add as much milk or water as required to form a firm dough. Cover this and keep aside for 15–20 minutes.

Prepare the sugar syrup by adding the sugar and water to a pan. On medium to low flame, cook till the sugar is dissolved. Turn off the heat and add the cardamom powder to the syrup.

Make little balls from the dough, make sure that there are no cracks in the dough balls. I add a few slivers of almonds into the centre of each ball—but it's not essential. Heat refined vegetable oil, or ghee, in a deep pan on medium heat. Once the oil is boiling hot, based on the size of your wok, drop a few dough balls into the oil and fry till they're golden brown. Make sure that the flame is on medium heat or the gulab jamun will remain uncooked in the centre and burn on the outside. Remove the gulab jamuns and place them in the bowl with sugar syrup for at least 30 minutes before serving. The gulab jamuns will practically double in size. Serve the gulab jamuns with the syrup.

Jalebi
Sweet Lord of the Rings

One of the best parts of walking to my grandfather's law chambers in Calcutta is the presence of multiple little food stalls—some in little grottos in the wall just large enough to fit the chef with pots of food around him, as he doles out his wares to hungry lawyers, law clerks, and clients. Then there's the man who has set up benches on the pavement, where people are served rice and fish curry or rice and egg curry in steel plates. The curry for both is the same, and based on your preference, a piece of fried fish or fried boiled egg is thrown into the spicy red gravy, which also has one large potato in it. If you're in the mood for a fried snack instead, there's a shingara shop and a kochuri-alu shop as well. Most of these stalls have already cooked their wares by early morning and remain busy serving the dish in patal bowls all day.

But there's one shop where the wares are prepared piping hot—the jalebi or jilipee shop. A large man, who seems immune to the unbearable heat of the city and his surroundings, sits over a large kadhai of boiling oil and squeezes out a creamy batter from a rustic piping bag made of muslin cloth. With the kind of ease only an expert would have, he forms multiple small concentric coils of batter, maybe two inches in diameter, which turn golden and crisp in the hot oil. He then fishes out the coils, which look like one large net of golden coils, breaks them up into individual coils with multiple rounds each, soaks them in the sugar syrup, removes the them before they lose their crisp bite, and serves them to the crowds standing around him. It's an intricate and dazzling process, and only the highly practised can make each concentric coil of jalebi the same shape as the last.

These golden-orange coils are crispy, a little chewy, and the dough inside has a sweet and molten centre to it. Jalebis are popular all across India; served in small sweetshops with rabri, paired with ice cream at fancy parties, and made hot for guests at weddings—I've even had apple jalebis at a nouvelle cuisine restaurant in Delhi. Jalebi can be very sweet or have just the right amount of sweetness.

Jalebi batter is usually made of flour, cardamom, saffron, and a fermenting agent. Sometimes, urad dal is added to the batter in the ratio of 75 per cent flour to 25 per cent dal. The batter is thin and traditionally poured into a muslin or linen cloth with a small hole pierced at its centre. This batter-filled muslin cloth is then squeezed from the top to form the concentric circles in boiling oil, moving from the innermost circle to the outermost. When the jalebis turn golden-brown, they are taken out and either soaked in a sugar syrup or brushed with sugar syrup before being served.

In India, it is quite common to have sweets for breakfast—in the same way that danishes, muffins, pancakes, and doughnuts are an integral part of breakfast in the West. In cities like Haridwar, Indore, and Calcutta people would eat jalebis as part of breakfast and sweetshops would start serving them early in the morning. The sweet also has multiple names including—but not limited to—jilbi, zelapi, jilipee, jilapir, jahangiri, and pak in West Asia. The imarti is a bigger and sweeter version of the jalebi with slightly different ingredients. The ingredients vary from region to region as well, as is expected. In parts of the country, the batter consists of urad dal and rice flour with a little chickpea flour and wheat flour. In other parts of the country, it includes semolina and baking powder. In Bengal, paneer and khoya is used.*

Although extremely popular in India, it does seem that the jalebi didn't originate here. The jalebi, as we know it, is a version of the West Asian zolabiya or zalabiya, which was introduced to India by Turkish and Persian traders and artisans. Jalebi is the local pronunciation of zalabiya. In Iran, zalabiya is served during festivals, especially at iftar gatherings during the holy month of

---

*Dileep Padgaonkar, 'Journey of the jalebi', *Times of India*, 15 March 2010.

Ramzan. In Lebanon, there is a pastry called zellabiya, that looks more like a churro without the grooves, and tastes similar to a jalebi. There are different versions of the jalebi in Turkey, Greece, and Cyprus, all with different local names. Interestingly, in Afghanistan, the sweet is served with fish in winter. According to Claudia Roden, one of the foremost authorities on Middle Eastern cookery, Egyptian jews also adapted zalabiya to celebrate Hanukkah.

So where did this transcontinental sweet actually take form first?

One of the earliest mentions of zalabiya can be found in the thirteenth-century Arab cookbook *Kitab al-Tabikh*. *Priyamkarnrpakatha*, a Jain text written by a scholar named Jinasura in 1450, mentions that jalebi was served at gatherings of rich merchants. Jalebi is again mentioned in the *Bhojana Kutuhala*, one of the Indian subcontinent's first books of recipes and food science written by Raghunatha in the seventeenth century. The recipe mentioned in the book is the one that is used even today. Another seventeenth-century Sanskrit 'cookery' book *Gunyagunabodhini* lists the ingredients and recipe of the sweet.

In fact, a paper written by the Indologist P. K. Gode in the *New Indian Antiquary* in 1943 explores the references to jalebi in both *Gunyagunabodhini*, which is written in Sanskrit verse, and *Priyamkarnrpakatha*. Even *The Oxford Companion to Food* states that the text by Jinasura mentions the jalebi while describing the delicacies served at a feast. *Priyamkarnrpakatha* has also been quoted extensively in cookery books published in later centuries such as the seventeenth-century classic, *Bhojana Kutuhala*, by Raghunatha.

Hobson-Jobson, a glossary of Anglo-Indian words which was first published in 1886, mentions that 'jalaubee' is 'apparently a corruption of the Arabic zalabiya or the Persian zilabiya'. *The Oxford Companion to Food* suggests that the original recipe of the sweet is mentioned in *Kitab al-Tabikh* and reiterates the theory that jalebi is originally an Iranian recipe for 'zoolabiya' or 'zulubiya', and was prepared on special occasions and distributed to the poor during the month of Ramzan.

Whichever shore it might have set sail from to reach India, the jalebi has found a great welcome here. The Indian version is thinner, crispier, and less sweet than its Middle Eastern cousins. We also don't use yeast as they do in the Middle East, and rarely use honey and rose water as they do in the Turkish version. And though these tiny differences don't make the jalebi necessarily better in India, they do make it more delectable for the Indian weather. Contrary to its convoluted concentric circles, the Indian jalebi is a simple celebration of dessert-making expertise, one that you can find both at small shops and at a high-end restaurant.

Daulat Ki Chaat
The Lingering Taste of Old Delhi

If there is any delicacy that can be associated with both New and Old Delhi, it is daulat ki chaat, which literally translates to 'the savoury that comes from wealth'. That this delicacy has as little to do with wealth as it has to do with being a savoury snack only adds to the enigma surrounding this sweet dish, which you can only sample on the streets of Delhi at the height of winter.

When I first moved to the capital, a decade or so ago, along with hearing about the wonders of the biryanis and kormas of Old Delhi—the mutton curry cooked with mince at Ashok & Ashok, the butter chicken at Kake Da Dhaba, kakoris at Al Kauser, and actual chaat at Chandni Chowk—the only sweet dish that I heard people sing paeans to was daulat ki chaat. I had to wait for eight months, through the sweltering heat of Delhi till a cold November made its appearance, because this sweet can only be prepared between the festivals of Diwali and Holi. What's more, I had to venture into Old Delhi, which looks charming in photographs, but is quite chaotic to wade through because of the crowds and traffic. At the sweet end of my journey, however, daulat ki chaat was so delicate and rich, if not wealthy, that it was worth the effort. It was almost soufflé like in its lightness and had just the right amount of sweetness. Mind you, daulat ki chaat cannot be packed for later consumption and is only found on the streets of Old Delhi early in the morning. By late morning, you can't find any daulat ki chaat—for love or for money! Urban legend has it that the sweet can only be prepared on a moonlit winter night.

One explanation for its curious name is that the 'daulat' in it comes from the foam used to make it, which froths right when the richest part of milk—the malai—forms before the milk comes to a boil. The term 'chaat' refers to the generous amounts of nuts and khoya sprinkled over it, in the same fashion that other garnishes are peppered over savoury chaats.

So what is this wonder, and did it live up to the drama that its name and the stories around it conjured up?

Daulat ki chaat is extremely light and airy. The sweet is prepared by churning thick, full-cream milk by hand till it becomes absolutely frothy. The topmost layer of the froth is lifted off the milk repeatedly, as lightly as possible, and placed in a separate bowl. Over this froth, a light sprinkling of powdered sugar and saffron-flavoured milk is drizzled. The myth about it being prepared only on cool, moonlit nights is not totally fanciful either. Unless the milk is absolutely cold and kept at the same temperature while being churned, the froth will not form properly. This is by far one of the lightest soufflés you can find, and it's truly astounding that it's whipped up by hand on a slab of ice that keeps the utensil it's being whipped in cool. And since this is a sweet made by street vendors in Old Delhi, and not in fancy restaurants with temperature-controlled dessert kitchens and refrigerators, it stands to reason that this delicate dessert can only be made in the dead of winter and early in the morning. It's such a delicate dish that as the day starts heating up, there's fear that the milk will turn sour. The moonlight is simply a touch of whimsy added to an already unbelievable delicacy.

I have to say that it is quite exciting to spot the sellers with their cane or wicker stands, called khomchas, or the younger lot with their pushcarts and ice slabs under the cart, carrying a large steel urn covered with a red cloth. For each serving, they dip into the cool urn, spoon out a very healthy portion of the whipped foam onto a plate made from dried sal leaves, top the foam with sugar, and depending on which cart or stand you've found, add some condensed milk or milk with saffron or dried fruits or khoya or a little drizzle of rose water and hand it over to you. A plate costs between forty and sixty rupees and you can buy a kilogram of daulat ki chaat for six hundred rupees. This is molecular gastronomy à la desi.

The process though, is an arduous one. According to

various daulat ki chaat sellers, whose experiences of cooking this dish are well-documented, the preparation for this dessert starts every evening around seven o'clock. This is when the first helping of cream is added to the milk before whisking begins. A thin muslin cloth is placed over the urn, which is then placed in the open under the cold night sky. According to its makers, this is the most critical step as the dew works on the milk overnight. At around four o'clock in the morning, a sprinkling of saffron is added to the milk, followed by vigorous churning by hand till froth starts forming on the surface. Adesh Kumar, who has run Khemchand Adesh Kumar's Daulat Ki Chaat for the last three decades, has been quoted as saying, 'This froth won't form if the milk is not placed under the open winter night sky.'*

There is no documentation of who actually created daulat ki chaat, and many theories have floated around over the years. Different versions can be found in other cities such as the malayo in Varanasi, malai makhan in Kanpur, and nimish in Lucknow. The origins of these sweets sound as fantastical as that of daulat ki chaat, and with a similarly tenuous link to fact. One of the credible stories in the canon is that the art of creating a unique dessert made with milk froth came to India with the Kyrgyz Botai tribe from Central Asia—one of the most ancient tribes of the region—which might have entered India during their journey through the Silk Route. The tribe, and its use of mare's milk to create a drink called kumis, is

---

*Asheesh Mamgain, 'If You Could Eat the Clouds... It Would Be Nimish/Daulat ki Chaat', *The Citizen*, 4 January 2019.

considered to be a part of daulat ki chaat's history.

According to historical accounts, mare's milk was greatly relished by the Botai because of its rich and smooth texture and flavour that no other dairy product possessed. This milk was used to create a fermented milk drink called kumis which used to be carried by men during expeditions. While preparing this, it is said that the cream had to be skimmed off the milk at regular intervals. According to the writings of the thirteenth-century monk William of Rubruck, who was the first European to visit the Mongol capital of Karakoram on the Orhon River and return to write about it, kumis was a prized drink and it was prepared in the following manner:

First, gallons of milk were collected and kept in a cool place. Once enough was collected, the milk was transferred to leather bags and then beaten. After the beating generated enough heat to pass through the skin of the leather bags, the milk inside would boil like new wine. The boiled milk would be churned regularly to collect all the butter, which was saved on the side. It was this butter that was served to the slaves and workers with a little honey and dry fruits. The rest of the milk was for kumis which, over a few days, developed the pungency of wine with an aftertaste of almond milk in a thinner consistency. He also explained that the Botai churned the milk until the thicker parts settled at the bottom, like dregs of wine, and the lightest part rose to the top, like whey or white mist.[*]

---

[*]Madhulika Dash, 'Culinary history: A journey called Daulat Ki Chaat', *bawarchi.com*, accessed on 7 October 2021.

This technique of churning milk to a foamy consistency and then harvesting its cream can also be seen in Andhra and Surat, which were known to be on the trading routes of the Mongols. This might also explain the Parsi concoction of cardamom-flavoured foam and milk called doodh na puff. Whether the technique moved from the coast to North India because of inter-kingdom trade or war is not clear. The first anecdotal mention of daulat ki chaat is around the same time as when the shahi tukda was recorded in the Mughal court. The original shahi tukda was supposedly made from layers of cream skimmed off boiling milk and placed on a brass tray. Once enough cream was collected, the tray was allowed to sit in a corner that was kept chilled with blocks of ice covered with jute. Once set, these layers took on a soft cheese-like consistency and were cut into bite-sized wedges. The earliest versions of the shahi tukda were prepared in a chilled room, much like daulat ki chaat, and were sprinkled with burra, or palm sugar, and slivers of nuts and dates.

Another story about the origins of daulat ki chaat points to some Gujarati traders who created it as a winter treat and introduced it to other parts of the country. Yet another version has it that it came from Kanpur during the making of Shahjahanabad. The addition of saffron, mawa, and dried fruits is reminiscent of other Mughal recipes, and explains the presence of makhan malai in Uttar Pradesh. Another version is that daulat ki chaat originated in the Awadhi kitchens of Kanpur under Saadat Ali Khan, the nawab of Awadh, who asked his khansamas to whip up a delicacy for the Mughal prince Murad Baksh.

Nowadays, to meet the demand for the sweet, daulat ki chaat sellers can be found even in the early evenings in Old Delhi. And if you'd rather not brave the labyrinthine lanes and crowds of Purani Dilli, you can trot over to Indian Accent at The Lodhi—the only restaurant that has mastered this delicacy thanks to a clever use of nitrogen combined with milk and cream—and truly pay a little chunk of your wealth for a serving garnished with fake five-hundred-rupee notes. In the heat of the summer, this is your only option if a craving for a little bite of heaven strikes.[*]

Even if we'll never know the true origins of this wonderfully light dessert, it is worth the effort to trudge into the innards of Old Delhi just to spot the daulat ki chaat seller and his khomcha, and taste a mouthful of Indian soufflé made under the moonlight—much like the Mongols and Mughals did hundreds of years ago.

---

[*]Chandni Sharma, 'How Do You Like Your Daulat Ki Chaat—Old School or High Tech?', *The Quint*, 16 October 2018.

DAULAT KI CHAAT

SERVES: 8   PREPARATION TIME: 12 HOURS

While daulat ki chaat is incredibly difficult to make at home, I have made nimish, a version of daulat ki chaat from Awadhi cuisine. It takes time, but the end result is brilliant.

INGREDIENTS

Milk	500 ml, full cream
Cream	100 ml, heavy
Cream of Tartar	½ tsp
Icing sugar	50 gm
Rose water	¼ tsp
Dried fruits	1 tbsp per serving

METHOD

Mix the milk, cream, and cream of tartar in a large bowl—I use a hand mixer. Cover and keep in the fridge overnight, or at least 12 hours. Remove the bowl from the fridge and immediately add the icing sugar and rose water.

Whisk the mixture at high speed. A layer of foam will form on top of the mixture, scoop it up and serve either in a large bowl or individual serving bowls. Sprinkle a little icing sugar. Keep repeating this till all the milk is over.

Garnish with pistachios and serve chilled.

Mishti Doi, Shrikhand, Bhapa Doi
Haute Culture Curd

Across India, with the notable exceptions of Bengal, Goa, and the northeastern states, meals are usually accompanied by a bowl of curd, which is often set at home. Growing up in Bengal, I'd never witnessed this practice. Curd was the backbone of our meals—our vegetables are cooked in it, as is our fish, mutton, and chicken—but we never served curd separately to complement a meal. It's odd that in Bengal we don't have an affinity for what we call 'tauk doi' or sour curd despite the obsession we have for mishti doi or sweet curd.

There is nary a single Bengali sweetshop within and beyond the border of Bengal which will not have clay urns of varying sizes, filled with perfectly-set and caramelized curd covered with thin paper and held together by a rubber band around the urn. Originating in West Bengal, mishti doi is made by reducing full cream milk over heat till it is half its quantity and then sweetening it with sugar cane or palm jaggery. After the milk has reduced and is sweetened, yoghurt is added to the bowl and left in a cool, dark place for the temperature and the yoghurt to work wonders.

Mishti doi is always served cold. In many old Bengali homes, you'll find heirloom stone and marble bowls that were designed to keep the mishti doi cold. But despite this and the limited ingredients, mishti doi is very rarely made at home. This is for two reasons. The first has to do with the fact that it takes a long time, and perfect conditions, to prepare. You need a cool, dark room in which to store the mixture to allow it to set. If you aren't careful, the mixture will either curdle or split. The second reason is pure laziness, reinforced by the fact that sweetshops have been selling delicious mishti doi for over 150 years. And so, the less troublesome option is to stop by your neighbourhood sweetshop and pick up an urn of mishti doi.

Some references suggest that the Dutch East India Company brought mishti doi to Bengal in the seventeenth century. Another theory suggests that mishti doi was a late nineteenth to early twentieth century creation. According to this theory, which finds favour with many culinary historians, a dairy farmer named Gouro Gopal Chandra Ghosh, from the Sherpur area of Bogra in present-day Bangladesh, created the recipe for mishti doi and began selling it as dessert. Legend has it that the then nawab of Bogra, Altaf Ali Chowdhury, bestowed Ghosh with land where he and two of his siblings set up a small cottage industry, which today produces about sixty thousand containers of curd every day across approximately fifty factories. The two oldest curd makers in Bogra—still standing strong—are Gouro Gopal Dodhi Bhandar and Ruchita Doi Ghor.

In Nabadwip, a version of the mishti doi is lal doi or red yoghurt. Like all good folklore about the origins of what we eat today, multiple histories exist that relate how and when this dessert was invented. But the one that seems to persist is that it was created by Kali Ghosh on this little island on the western bank of the Bhagirathi in West Bengal. Ghosh, along with his brother Hari, used to make curd and whey. The mishti doi made by this family is known as lal doi because of its colour. According to a news report in the Bengali newspaper *Anandabazar Patrika*, the brothers used to simmer buffalo milk for hours, slowly adding water to the mixture, till it lost all its water content and became condensed milk. The slow cooking would give the milk a red hue. The whey produced from this milk is called lal ghol or red whey. Lal doi is also referred to as chaku doi because the yoghurt is so thick that it doesn't fall out of its urn when upended. Even a knife, or chaku, lodged in this yoghurt will not fall down when turned over. I have only heard and read of this, but never seen it put to the test, though I don't see a reason why I shouldn't get cracking on this soon.

Another avatar is made by the 150-year-old Lakkhi Narayan Mistanna Bhandar in Nabadwip, which produces the best kheer doi in town. It is called kheer doi because of the consistency of the yoghurt, which is slowly cooked over a simmering flame for over six hours till the milk is reduced to half. After a laborious six hours, the makers add sugar and simmer the milk overnight. The next morning, this mixture is stored in clay urns, which are gently moved from time to time till the curd has set. It is impossible to know every method that exists when it comes to making different mishti dois—Jadhav Chandra Das, a Calcutta sweetshop established in 1858, produces a sparkling white mishti doi but is very protective of its recipe.

Bhapa doi is one of the more recent versions of mishti doi, which is found in very few sweetshops because it requires a double boiler to prepare, one that isn't of much use in other Bengali sweets. This was also the only Bengali dessert my grandmother used to bother making at home. Bhapa doi is a steamed version of mishti doi, which isn't as sweet and has a cheesecake-like consistency to it. Bhapa doi, or Bengal's answer to cheesecake, is often flavoured with saffron and cardamom, and sometimes topped with mango puree.

Across the subcontinent, Gujarat is known for the only other yoghurt-based dessert in India. Shrikhand is prepared from hung curd, which is delicately flavoured with saffron, cardamom, and dried fruit. The consistency is that of mascarpone cheese or parfait. The key to a perfect shrikhand lies in the length of time you hang the curd in a muslin cloth, to drain as much water as possible from it. The difference between shrikhand and bhapa doi is that the former doesn't need to be baked or steamed. It is also often served with a savoury puri or flatbread, which makes for an interesting sweet-and-savoury dish.

Shrikhand can be traced back to 400 BCE. According to the book *The History of Fermented Foods* by Jashbhai B. Prajappati and Baboo M. Nair, shrikhand originated in ancient India and may be considered 'one of the oldest desserts to originate on Indian shores.' In *The Historical Dictionary of Indian Food*, K. T. Achaya traces the shrikhand to 500 BCE and writes, 'To dewater curd, it was hung in a muslin bag for a few hours; sugar and spices added to the mass yielded shikharini (identical with modern day shrikhand), first noted around 500 BCE.' According to him, it is the modern version of shikharini, or shikhrini, which was eaten by people in what is present-day Gujarat and Maharashtra. The recipe for shrikhand and shikharini is the same, and finds mention in Gujarati-Jain literature from the seventh to the fourteenth centuries. In what seems to be an inescapable and inevitable fate for most desserts, even shrikhand is now prepared with mango and other fruits, although Sindhi and Gujarati cuisines have always had sweet and savoury mango recipes. Mango shrikhand is incredibly popular across sweetshops and Indian restaurants.

It's surprising that there aren't more yoghurt-based Indian desserts given that, according to various food historians such as Achaya, the importance of curd in Indian cuisine dates back to the era of the Rig Veda. The text mentions that during Vedic times, curd was eaten as an accompaniment to rice.

By 1000 CE, curd was a common fixture in cooking, as

can be seen in traditional delicacies with historical pasts. That curd was created and eaten with such gusto across India isn't surprising when you realize its health and digestive benefits. Because temperatures are so high across the year, you need cooling foods to deal with the heat. This is why curd is usually eaten with rice or roti, or eaten after a meal. While the presence of good bacteria in curd might not have been known to people in 400 BCE, the antibiotic properties of curd, thanks to the bacteria which turns milk into yoghurt, could not have gone unnoticed. This is also why you will find very few traditional recipes which require you to heat or cook yoghurt. But raitas, pachdis, plain yoghurt, chaach, and chaat with spiced dahi have all remained extremely popular for centuries.

The only other state which has a yoghurt-based dessert is Assam, which serves creamy yoghurt drizzled with jaggery as a simple end to a meal—a nod to how simple and yet sublime yogurt is.

Whether it is mishti doi, bhapa doi, or shrikhand, I find it fascinating that in a country which had no concept of ovens or bain-maries, we've produced desserts such as bhapa doi and shrikhand in kitchens at home.

BHAPA DOI/BAKED YOGHURT

SERVES: 8   PREPARATION TIME: 15 MINUTES, 24 HOURS TO SET

INGREDIENTS

Natural yoghurt	500 gms, low fat
Condensed milk	400 gms
Green cardamom	4 pods
Saffron	10-12 strands, soaked in of milk
Cashews and Pistachios to garnish	

METHOD

Preheat the oven to 190°C. Roast the cardamom in a large shallow baking tray in the oven for about 5 minutes. Heat the milk with saffron strands in the microwave for 10 seconds and leave until later. In the meantime, mix yogurt and condensed milk together until smooth. Crush the cardamom pods and stir them into the yogurt mix. Add ⅔ of the chopped nuts as well.

Fill a baking dish with the yoghurt mixture. Place the baking dish in a large and shallow baking tray. Fill this tray with enough hot water to submerge at least half of the smaller dish. Then carefully place the whole tray in the oven for 10 minutes. After this, sprinkle some strands of saffron and a little bit of the saffron milk on top of the yoghurt. Sprinkle a few of the nuts as well. Bake for another 5 minutes until the yoghurt has set.

Leave for 10 minutes, or until it cools down, and then refrigerate. Always serve bhapa doi chilled.

Goan Sweets
Gems from an Indigenous Pastelaria

Vindaloo. Sorpotel. Beaches. Shacks. Sun. Sand. Sea. Nights of hectic partying. Days filled with shopping, visiting churches, and trying different cuisines. The Russian mafia. Taking a cruise on the Mandovi River. Drinking and then cooking with feni. Oh! The seafood and the steaks! To say nothing of the pearl Goan sausages made in a small Goan village. There's so much you hear about Goa, but unless you're a bona fide Goan or a food connoisseur, no one mentions that Goa is the only state that has a variety of desserts and sweets which are totally unique to the locale—unlike other states which share different versions of the same preparation or delicacy. These sweets are unlike any other Indian confections—they use procedures and recipes that are foreign to the rest of the country.

For over 450 years, Goa was a Portuguese territory. What is known as Portuguese India, or Estado da Índia Portuguesa, came into being six years after the discovery of a sea route between the Indian subcontinent and Portugal. After 1510, Goa became the capital of the Portuguese viceroyalty and remained under Portuguese rule until 1961, although Portugal only recognized the Indian reabsorption of Goa in 1974 after a treaty was signed.

While other port towns and cities had French, British, Dutch, and Danish settlers—none of them left a lasting imprint on the local cuisine as the Portuguese did. In Goa, the Portuguese imprint on Goan cuisine is visible in the wonderful union of cooking ingredients, processes, and delicacies between the local and imported Iberian traditions.

To give credit where it is due, we must thank the Portuguese traders for introducing Goa and India to a large number of ingredients that are now culinary staples in many of our kitchens. Corn, potatoes, tomatoes, cashews, custard apples, guavas, cocoa, papayas, peanuts, vanilla, sweet potatoes, and oyster mushrooms, all came to India with the Portuguese. Arguably the most important ingredient used across the country, chillies were brought here by the Portuguese. Till the eighteenth century, chillies were available only in the Konkan region, and were called 'pernambuco peppers' after the northeastern state of Brazil that borders Bahia.[*]

---

[*] Vivek Menezes, 'Goa's Best Chef is a Secret', *Livemint*, 18 January 2020.

Along with chillies and other ingredients we swear by today, the Portuguese also introduced culinary preparations common to both Goa and Lisbon in present times. The Portuguese presence in Goa left an indelible mark on the shared culinary heritage across the two cultures. In fact, Portuguese dishes are mainstays of home-cooked meals to this day. And the repertoire of sweets is as wide as it is delectable.

Cakes, marzipans, crepes, and biscuits are common in traditional Goan households but foreign to Indian kitchens. According to the census, 25 per cent of Goans are Christian, while 66 per cent are Hindu. The Christian population is almost entirely Roman Catholic, and Goan Catholics form a significant ethno-religious group. However, a certain kind of syncretism marks celebrations in the state—sweets created by Christians for their festivals are adapted by Hindu households for their festivities.

Unsurprisingly, a connecting thread that runs through the surfeit of sweets prepared in Goa is the use of coconut. It is almost impossible to find a sweet which doesn't use grated coconut and Goan palm jaggery. Almost as impossible as it is to find a lane in Goa which doesn't have a coconut tree providing some respite from the sun.

You keep hearing about the usual suspects: dodo, bebinca, and so on. But when you go to Goa, always ask a local to recommend a dessert—exactly what I did on one of my trips there. As a result, I was introduced to one of my favourite Goan desserts, the serradura. It is that rare Goan dessert that doesn't use coconut. More interestingly, it's a popular Macanese dish that travelled to Goa from another one of Portugal's colonies. Macanese cuisine itself is a blend of Chinese and Portuguese cuisines created by the wives of Portuguese sailors who attempted to replicate European flavours in the erstwhile colony of Macau. Macanese cuisine is also a testament to the strength of Portuguese maritime influence in the sixteenth and seventeenth centuries. We can also trace African, Indian, and Malaccan influences in Macanese recipes and cooking styles today. The cuisine is known for using ingredients such as coconut milk, cloves, and cinnamon which are closely associated with Konkani preparations. Back to serradura, which I first tasted at a fancy hotel in Goa, after a Goan chef recommended it.

Where do I begin? Serradura is a multi-layered chilled dessert, also known as sawdust pudding because of the biscuit crumbs in it. The Macanese version of the dessert uses Bolacha Maria cookies, which are the freshly baked version of what we call Marie biscuits in India. This dessert is incredibly simple to prepare—it consists of layers of chilled whipped cream and crumbled Bolacha Maria cookies. It's the best kind of dessert—simple in flavour, but extremely delicious and lovely to look at; usually served in a trifle bowl.

Not a fan of cream? You could always try Goa's local answer to crepes. Lent is a period of fasting for some Christians and Shrove Tuesday, which precedes Ash Wednesday in the run-up to Lent, marks the day when Christians clear their kitchen cabinets of eggs, milk, and fat. For the same purpose, Goan Christians prepare a dessert called alle belle for Shrove Tuesday. Alle belle is a crepe stuffed with freshly grated coconut and Goan palm jaggery. It's a lot like the Bengali patishapta or the Keralite mutta palada. Most traditional Goan homes will serve you alle belle if you visit for tea.

The baath cake is another favourite from the days between Christmas and Easter. Soft, moist, and very close to a tres leche cake, the baath cake is a celebration of all things coconut. It uses coconut oil, coconut milk, and coconut cream. The cake is prepared with coconut, condensed milk, and semolina and flavoured with rose water which gives it a particularly nutty flavour. It's an extremely moist and tender cake which is easy to prepare. The key to getting the baath cake right is to allow the batter to sit overnight—this results in fluffy and fragrant semolina that has absorbed all the coconut oil and milk.

It's not all cakes and biscuits in Goa. Goan doss, or doce de grao, is a fudge-like dessert which you can find easily in almost any bakery in Goa. 'Doce' means sweet and 'grao' means grain in Portuguese. What's impressive is that practically every dessert in Goa uses very few ingredients. Also, every ingredient is easily available and affordable. Goan desserts eschew saffron, raisins, and expensive dry fruits for local ingredients such as coconuts and cashews. The doce de grao is made with split gram dal, grated coconut, sugar, and ghee. The dal and coconut is pureed separately into a thick paste without water, after which it is mixed with sugar and ghee, and slow-cooked to form a light brown paste which is cooled and cut into diamond-shaped pieces. Doce is always prepared during Christmas, or at weddings and special occasions.

Another Christmas specialty, which is similar to a hard-textured coconut barfi, is cocada or kokad. This, however, is prepared with fine semolina and coconut, and is white in colour. The history of the cocada is far more complicated than its preparation. Cocada can be traced back to nineteenth-century Spain. The word 'cocada' is derived from coconut and the Spanish suffix of 'ada' means 'a hit' or 'a strike'. The suffix 'ada' usually indicates the act of striking something with a sharp object, in this case cracking open a coconut.

There are many variants of cocadas in Spain and Latin America—in coastal areas and inland—and these are extremely popular in Mexico, Argentina, Chile, Uruguay, Colombia, Ecuador, and Peru. Cocadas are primarily made with freshly grated or ground coconut and then cooked with sugar, with slight differences across Latin America. There are also sources that document that cocadas were sold in many Spanish and Latin American pastry shops as early as 1890. And now, thanks to the Portuguese, you can find them in practically every local sweetshop in Goa.

From barfis to desserts wrapped in steamed leaf parcels, the range of sweets you get in Goa is as diverse as its beaches. And just like the beaches, some sweets are more popular than others. Then there are the hidden gems that only the locals know of, such as the Goan patholi or patoleo. This dessert is prepared by making a paste with red rice, coconut, jaggery, and raisins which is then wrapped in turmeric leaves and steamed.

Goan patoleo is prepared during special occasions, and is always prepared on the day marking the Solemnity of the Assumption of the Virgin Mary and for the São João Feast. Patoleo's main ingredient, turmeric leaves, is in abundance during the monsoon season. Goan families also prepare this as a teatime snack, and it goes by many names from patoleo to patoli.

Now onto the one dessert which Goa is synonymous with, the multi-layered bebinca. Traditionally, the dessert is made of seven thin, gelatinous layers of batter made from eggs, flour, coconut milk, and sugar, and flavoured with ghee, nutmeg, and cardamom. Bebinca can take up to six hours or more to cook since each layer needs to be baked separately and in quick succession.

In her book, *Cozinha de Goa*, Fatima da Silva Gracia writes that the bebinca could have been invented by Bibiona, a nun at the Convento da Santa Monica in Old Goa. Bibiona's version had seven layers to represent the seven hills of Lisbon and Old Goa.[*] She offered it to a priest who felt it wasn't impressive enough, after which versions of bebinca were prepared with more layers. Silva Gracia also mentions that the word 'bebinca' is used for other unlayered desserts such as bebinca de claras which uses egg whites left over from the regular bebinca—waste not, want not. The use of egg yolks in bebinca is what makes it typically

---

[*]Ashwin Rajagopalan, 'Why Bebinca is Known as the Queen of Goan Desserts', *NDTV Food*, 18 May 2016.

Portuguese. The potato bebinca or bebinca de batata is also an extremely popular local version which isn't baked in layers and uses potatoes in the mixture. That the Portuguese took bebinca with them to all their colonies is evident from the fact that there were versions of the dessert in another Portuguese colony, Mozambique in East Africa. In 2006, when Macau received the dubious privilege of naming an Asian storm, they christened it bebinca. The name is also used elsewhere in Asia—in Malaysia and the Philippines—but usually in reference to layered desserts, not storms. Although bebinca is quintessentially Goan, there is a similarity to the Dutch-Indonesian cake called spekkoek or lapis legit, which means 'layered stickiness'. In *Curry: A Tale of Cooks and Conquerors*, British historian Lizzie Collingham writes about the bebinca's transnational roots: 'Bebinca travelled with the Portuguese to Malaya and from there to the Philippines, where the cooks dispensed with the time-consuming layers. From the Philippines, bebinca continued on its extraordinary journey to Hawaii, where it transmuted to butter mochi, a fudge-like rice-flour dessert.'* A simpler dessert, when it comes to its antecedents as well, is the Goan pinaca or pinagr. Shaped like rissoles, pinaca is another sweet made with coconut, palm jaggery, and plump Goan parboiled red rice. A cooked log is made from these ingredients, which is chopped up and rolled into croquettes and served.

Another favourite which you will rarely, if ever, see on a restaurant menu is bol which resembles a half shell of a

---

*Menezes, 'Goa's Best Chef is a Secret'.

coconut. Bol is traditionally prepared during weddings. Two days before a Goan wedding ceremony, a basket containing bol, doce, and bananas is sent by the bride's family to the groom's family as part of the wedding trousseau. Bols are baked hard jaggery cakes which are prepared from coarse wheat, jaggery, coconut, cardamom powder, toddy, and salt. Another feature of Goan desserts is that you won't find an authentic Goan dessert that is liquid or semi-liquid. Goan desserts use ingredients and processes that have a long shelf life, which was clearly developed keeping the heat and humidity of the region in mind.

Goan lapsi is yet another dessert served at teatime, which explains why Goans love their siesta and tend to be as sedentary as Bengalis. Broken wheat is cooked in coconut milk to prepare this porridge-like pudding. You won't find this in sweetshops, so you'd need to visit a Goan home to taste it.

The sweet which I find very unique is the tavsali—an eggless steamed cucumber cake. Tavsali gets its name from the Konkani word 'tavshe' which means cucumber. Cucumber, jaggery, broken wheat, semolina, grated coconut, cashews, and raisins are cooked on low heat in a thick-bottomed pan on indirect heat—a cooking technique which is not the norm in India. And if you're not in the mood for cucumber, you can always opt for dhonus, which allows you to substitute cucumbers with jackfruit.

The one sweet which you find in Hindu Maharashtrian homes as well is the nevri, which is known popularly as karanji.

This is prepared during Christmas by the Christians and during Ganesh Chaturthi and Diwali by the Hindus. These sweet crescent-shaped dumplings made of flour are stuffed with a coconut, sugar, poppy seeds, cardamom, and almond mixture, and then fried. It's not clear whether Maharashtrian Hindus picked it up from Goan Christians or not, but the similarity between karanji and nevri is uncanny. The Christians make this for Christmas and add jaggery and coconut to the mixture. Like most local dishes in any part of the world, every home has its own version.

This, of course, is not an exhaustive list of all the Goan sweets you can find, but a census would be too long to be included in its entirety. I've chosen my favourites and the ones with the most interesting flavours and history. There are, of course, the bolinhas—coconut biscuits you'll find in every bakery shop in Goa. Not to mention other desserts such as kul kul, kokisan, coconut ice, and egg tarts—the exact replica of which is the pastel de nata, a local delicacy in Portugal.

Whether it's the use of marzipan, or unconventional techniques or the obsession with biscuits—what makes Goan sweets worth mentioning in detail is that they have retained these traditions across multi-ethnic homes in the region. It's a testament to the lasting impact that the Portuguese had on Indian cuisine—whether it be the ingredients we've grown to accept as commonplace and even indigenous to India, or the Goan delicacies which one can find in far off regions of the world. I would strongly advise visiting a local Goan bakery shop next time you're in the state, and working your way through the sweets. You're unlikely to find them anywhere else in India, after all.

Firinghee Sweets
Delicious Relics of the Raj

There are two desserts that we grew up eating in Calcutta—one was a treat, and seemed a little magical when we were growing up and knew nothing of the science of baking, and the other was commonplace, turning up not just at our dining table but also at many homes I visited in Calcutta and across the clubs of the city.

The first was the Baked Alaska, the antecedents of which seem to be most confusing, and the second is caramel custard. At Calcutta's Sky Room, which was opened in 1957 and shut in 1993, you could take a step back in time and enjoy some of the finest dining the city had to offer. Chilled prawn cocktail in silver prawn cocktail servers, which kept the prawn and Marie

Rose sauce chilled with the crushed ice at the bottom of the serving dish, or the freshly baked Biscotti—not available for love or money in any other bakery in the city in those years—followed by your choice of steak, grilled pork chops, smoked hilsa, and any other dish you can think of.

But the end of the meal was the piece de resistance—a dessert trolley laden with individual portions of the most perfect and jiggly caramel custard, black forest cake, and that magical dessert known to us as Baked Alaska.

The Baked Alaska is a fabulous creation made of ice cream covered in meringue, which is flambéed right at your table. Cutting into what looks like an obviously hot dessert, diners are thrilled to find perfectly chilled ice cream at the centre. It really seemed like magic as a child, and Baked Alaska is one of the most fantastical desserts for kids—mixing a bit of showmanship with ice cream. Now that I know a smattering of physics and the science of baking, it's still very impressive.

According to an NPR podcast I heard on the creation of Baked Alaska, the dessert belongs to the kitchens of both the French and the Americans. Baked Alaska, as it is called, was invented in the eighteenth century by the American-born British scientist Sir Benjamin Thompson. Thompson is also behind the life-saving inventions of a kitchen range and a double boiler, so god bless his soul. He had made the discovery that the air bubbles inside whipped egg whites made meringue an insulator, which is why the ice cream doesn't melt when covered in swirls of this cloudy delight. The dessert was named after Alaska, which the United States of America bought from Russia in 1867.

But cuisine in Calcutta and India is not known for its American influence—unless we want to place the creation of the American chopsuey and its entry into India at America's doorstep. Baked Alaska, which you now get at various other restaurants in Calcutta, namely Peter Cat, could well have found its way to our dining tables via the French.

The Franco-American dessert was preceded in the 1830s by a dessert called the omelette norvegienne created by French chefs. This version is made up of alternate layers of cake and ice cream, which is then covered in meringue and broiled. The French named this dessert after Norway. The first instance of this dessert's recipe can be found in the 1894 cookbook *The Epicurean* which was written by Charles Ranhofer, an expat Parisian pastry chef who worked at Delmonico's restaurant in New York City, and was known for his culinary creations. It's called the Alaska, Florida in his book. Interestingly, Delmonico is still standing today and so is its Baked Alaska.

Larousse Gastronomique, the final word in cooking, published in 1938 and compiled by the French chef Prosper Montagné, mentions an omelette surprise which uses the same ingredients as a Baked Alaska. 'A sponge cake soaked in syrup, ice cream, and meringue—but with the addition of fruit. The base which may be Genoa cake, Genoese sponge, or madeleine cake mixture is sprinkled with liquer, covered with a bombe mixture, a fruit ice cream or a parfait mixture, mixed with preserved fruits or praline violets. The entire is then masked with meringue and glazed in the oven. The dessert is surrounded by poached fruits or cherries in brandy.' In Sky Room or Blue Fox and now at Peter Cat, Baked Alaska is simply doused in rum or brandy and flambéed and brought to the table enveloped in a blue flame.

Who do we thank for this creation—which honestly looks better than it tastes? The French or the Americans, I cannot say.

That other dessert which has strong Anglo-Indian, and clear British and French influences is the caramel custard. You get it at the oddest of restaurants and almost every patisserie worth its salt. This custard was made religiously across homes I visited and still visit—given that it's one of the easiest desserts to prepare when it comes to the ingredients or the utensils and baking paraphernalia required to prepare it. I am assuming that the memsahibs and their khansamas realized that this was not just easy to prepare but also required minimum effort. Milk, eggs, and sugar were whisked together and even in the absence of an oven, could be prepared in a double boiler on a stove top.

The creme caramel is a slightly richer version of the caramel custard, which we are used to. But you can link the creation of the caramel custard back to the custard and the caramel. Caramel custard might be popular in India because it is similar in texture to many Indian desserts and doesn't use flour or have the consistency of cake. You don't even need to add butter to make it. But what a delight it is when served swimming in a pool of caramel.

Another dessert which can be found across country clubs in India is the soufflé. Lemon soufflé, chocolate soufflé, orange soufflé—name it and any country club will have at least one version on their menu. Cold, light, and very tasty if cooked well, the soufflé is impossible to make without the right weather and paraphernalia. Which is why it's a marvel that it was made in India way before air conditioners and refrigeration must have been commonplace.

Clearly brought to our shores by the French, according to *The Calcutta Cookbook*, 'It was usual for Viceroys of India to bring in their entourage, an English butler, a French or English lady's maid, and a French chef. A team of Indian cooks worked in the viceregal kitchens under the supervision of a French chef.'

Creating the perfect soufflé is a tedious process. You need to whip egg whites separately till they make peaks—imagine doing this without an electric beater! Then beat egg yolks and sugar, add gelatin, set this in a fridge, then add the egg whites and whatever flavouring you're using, and then leave it to set in the fridge—and pray that it doesn't fall flat because you haven't whipped it well enough or because you've whipped it too much.

That these desserts, which were made in the cool climes of France, were replicated in hot and humid cities like Calcutta, Chennai, Pondicherry, Chandannagore, and Delhi is testament to the genius of the khansamas who were trained by the memsahibs in these Anglo-Indian homes, and in the homes of the brown sahibs who had returned from studying or working in 'vilayet' and wanted to eat firinghee food and a pudding after dinner.

The steam pudding is definitely one of those creations which we can thank the burrasahibs and their Bihari Muslim, Dacca Christian, and Barua Mog khansamas for—the holy trinity that reigned supreme in Indian kitchens of the memsahibs and the bhadralok.

The other favourite which most don't even realize has nothing to do with Indian desserts but has become utterly commonplace is the cake.

Each of the colonizers and trading countries brought in their version of cake, which was adopted lovingly by the Indian state they entered. The Goan Bolo Sans Rival can be found in Portugal, as I discovered when I visited the country. Bolo means cake in Portuguese, and this version of cake uses semolina instead of flour. Goa also has the baath cake which is similar to the bolo, but uses coconut powder as one of its main ingredients. They even have a cashew cake with buttercream. The baath cake, while introduced to Goan kitchens by the Portuguese settlers, actually has a connection to the basbousa which is a 'water-cake' prepared in Egypt with semolina and orange blossom water.

If you walk into any Irani restaurant or bakery in Mumbai or Pune, you'll notice little cupcakes made from dried whole milk or mava, and without eggs. They are topped with either almond flakes or cardamom. Another cake I discovered only when I shifted to Delhi was the milk cake which is less cake and more mithai but is sold as cake. The concept of cake is so commonplace in India that this sweet, which is essentially a kalakand though it faintly resembles a cake, is popularly referred to as cake.

The one truly Anglo-Indian dessert which has permeated every colonial-era boarding school in India is the bread pudding. If you don't have cake or the ingredients for cake, this is perfect. This combination of faux cake and custard, the bread pudding, has been served ad nauseum in school dinners for donkey's years and in cafeterias which want to serve you a pudding, but want to make it as economical as possible. All you need is stale bread, milk, eggs, and sugar and there you have it. I make a version with chocolate chips and rum, which is a souped up version of a bread and butter pudding.

Another school and club favourite, which was introduced by the British is the roly-poly or suet pudding. Now this you rarely see on menus anymore and if you do, the suet is replaced by butter, which definitely won't give you the same texture or taste. Suet is the hard fat of beef, lamb, or mutton found around the animal's loins and kidneys. For a suet pudding, this is mixed with flour, breadcrumbs, sugar, eggs, and milk to form a dough which is placed on a wet cloth in a flat rectangle. This dough is topped with jam, and rolled up like a Swiss roll, wrapped in cloth, and then steamed for a couple of hours in a double boiler, after which it is unwrapped, sliced, and served with custard or jam. I really haven't seen an authentic roly-poly pudding in decades now.

Another dessert which was created to use easily available ingredients is the trifle. Stale cake (you really shouldn't be wasting good cake on a trifle), cream, jam, a little wine or sherry or rum, and custard are simply placed in successive layers to be chilled and served.

This is one of the greatest contributions of the Anglo-Indian kitchen. Not the cakes, or the cookies, or the puddings themselves, but the ability to innovate, to be frugal yet creative, and to come up with cooking procedures that beat the sweltering heat in India. There was no room for wasting stale bread, cake, and fat. You just came up with creative ways of turning it all into a sweet dish which wouldn't spoil in the Indian summer. We have much to thank the frugal firinghee kitchen for.

This is my favourite recipe for Bread Pudding with Dark Chocolate Chips. I saw it on one of Nigella Lawson's shows, but decided to be frugal and add my own cheap (but tasty) twist to it.

BREAD PUDDING WITH CHOCOLATE CHIPS

SERVES: 8   PREPARATION TIME: 50 MINUTES

INGREDIENTS

Stale bread	300 gms
Chocolate chips	200 gms
Brown eggs	3, large
Brown sugar	40 gms
Full fat cream	125 ml (I use Amul cream)
Full cream milk	500 ml
Granulated sugar	4 tsp
Dark rum	2 tbsp

METHOD

Preheat the oven to 170°C. Grease an ovenproof dish with butter. Mix the bread cubes and chocolate chips and place in the baking dish evenly.

Beat the eggs, brown sugar, cream, milk, and finally the rum. Pour this mixture over the bread and press the cubes down to coat them in the liquid. Let it soak for 15–20 minutes. Sprinkle some sugar on top (this gives it a nice brown colour and crunch) and bake in the oven for 50–60 minutes.

The pudding will puff up and you know you should take it out when you touch the bread and see that it wobbles slightly. You can serve immediately or later, but it should be served warm.

In God's Name
Sweetmeats and Cultural Congeniality

Religion in India has never been a private matter. Therefore it only follows that religious celebrations and festivities aren't private matters either. But in a good way, a few years ago, festivals across religions were part of a shared heritage. In a country that has about thirteen festivals in twelve months—and that's a very modest estimate—it was heartening to see how festival sweets cut across cultures and communities. It was a time when people, even the most devout, forgot about divisions and whether their gods were more equal than yours, and opened their homes and kitchens to everyone.

One of my favourite sweets, which is always served as a holy offering during Durga Pujo, Kali Pujo, Saraswati Pujo, and the many other festivals are these little balls of sugar, called Nokul Dana. They're tiny little opaque sugar balls that are always kept at the altar next to the gods. Another favourite of mine is the batasha—an affordable, small, and solid coin-shaped sugar confectionary. You can even get these made with jaggery, and they're the perfect way to ensure that children sit through unending prayers and rituals, just for the sugar high at the end of it.

Each festival and each community has its own prasad or holy offering to the gods and goddesses. But what is interesting to note is that over time, communities have started adopting each other's sweet dishes and sometimes creating their own versions of it. The whole lot—Eid, Diwali, Durga Puja, and others—will always have some popular sweets; some distinctly cultural sweets; and some that mark the harvest festivals of Pongal, Makar Sankranti, and Onam, amongst others, and use seasonal produce. Whether it is a Hindu household's version of the seviyan, or Muslims serving gulab jamun or rasgulla at Eid, or Gujaratis wanting a box of sandesh or mishti doi—a love for all kinds of sweets is clearly evident in these celebrations.

In Bengal, each day of the Durga Puja is marked by different sweets which are prepared specifically on that day. On Ashtami, or the eighth day, which is considered one of the most significant days in the worship of goddess Durga, kheer is made across homes, rich or poor. While any home can make an indulgent version of kheer, its warmth lies in a simple preparation of sweetened milk that evaporates and thickens over a low flame. Komola kheer, which uses tangerines from the first crop, is often prepared as well. The fruit is peeled and stirred into the cool kheer, and eaten with puffed bread or luchi most often. Kheer represents an age-old tradition and must have originated because of the need to preserve and utilize excess milk in the days before refridgerators.

Families usually pull out all the stops on the evening of Bijaya Dashami when the idols are to be submerged for the final ritual of bhashan. Through the evening, relatives and friends visit each other's houses exchanging sweets. The most common, of course, is the sandesh, but pantua, rajbhog, and rosogollas are popular as well.

One of the few sweets I saw even my grandmother and the cook make was the patishapta, which is unique to Bengal. It is the Bengali version of stuffed crepes. While it looks quite complicated and fancy, it's actually quite simple to make. Freshly grated coconut is mixed with gur or jaggery and cooked in a pan over medium flame. After about ten minutes of stirring the mixture, you get a fragrant mixture which is cooled. The crepes use flour, sugar, and some oil to create a thick batter. The pan is usually smeared with oil with the discarded stem of a brinjal which is dipped in oil, using the flat end of the stem to coat the pan with a layer of oil. The crepe batter is then poured to make a circle and when cooked, the coconut-jaggery mixture is placed in the middle with two sides of the crepe folded over it in an envelope. The crepe is then flipped continuously till both sides are slightly brown. You must believe you are a special guest when any home serves you patishapta with a spoonful of kheer drizzled over it.

The other sweet which is often made on Bijaya Dashami, the tenth day of Durga Pujo, is the malpoa—a flat, thick, round fennel-seed flavoured dough soaked in syrup. The syrup the malpoa is soaked in is of the utmost importance as it shouldn't be too thin. The syrup is made not just with water and sugar, but also with a teaspoon of lemon juice. The dumplings are made by mixing flour, peanut oil, milk, and a sprinkling of fennel seeds. This batter is then deep-fried till the malpoa is a dark burnt shade of caramel and the edges are curled up. Once it is fried, the malpoa is dipped into syrup and then served on a dish with more of the syrup drizzled over it.

This should explain the general portliness and constant indigestion faced by Bengalis. A version of the malpua is also found in Rajasthan. The Rajasthani malpua is made with chhana, sugar, ground nutmeg, cornflour, saffron, ghee, almond, and pistachio. It's a lighter shade than the Bengali malpua, but no less tasty.

An east Bengal speciality which is made on Shab-e-Barat, the night of destiny, is bread with different kinds of halwa. Shab-e-Barat is believed to be the night when god writes the destinies of everyone for the coming year based on their past deeds. The devout offer prayers, recite from the Quran, and perform religious rituals through the night of Shab-e-Barat. Most families also make excess bread to hand out to the less privileged on this day. The halwa can be made of carrots, flour, arrowroot, ground chana dal, carrots, gourds, and even meat or eggs.

The dimer halwa, which I find the most unique of the lot, is made with eggs, sugar, evaporated milk, ghee, cardamom, cinnamon, and saffron. Whipped eggs are mixed with all the other ingredients and then cooked in a pan on low heat. As soon as the mixture becomes granular and dry, it is removed from the heat, mixed with dried fruits and served.

Another version of this, that Chitrita Banerji writes of in *The Life and Food in Bengal,* is a barfi made with eggs. In this preparation, the whites and yolks of the eggs are separated and the whites are beaten till they are stiff. The yolks are whipped separately and then both are mixed together with sugar and ghee and heated and flavoured with either saffron or rose water or both. This mixture is stirred constantly and cooked till it starts sticking to the pan, and is then placed in a flat tray and allowed to cool completely before being cut into diamond-shaped barfis.

Speaking of sweets revered by the Muslim community in Bengal, the sweet dishes prepared on Eid-ul-Fitr, which marks the end of Ramzan, are not restricted to halwa or shahi tukda. Barfis, gulab jamuns, sandesh, and rasmalai are common fare. Both are prepared at home and offered to guests when they visit.

Another sweet which cuts across regions is the much loved pitha, which makes an appearance in winter during the Poush season. Pitha refers to all sweets made with rice, wheat, and coconut. Pitha was usually made by the womenfolk in joint families. One of the simplest but most unique variants of this sweet is made from kalai dal or urad dal. A paste of dal is whipped till frothy and then made into round balls which are deep-fried and dipped into a sweet syrup. The chitoi pitha, another version, is made from rice flour which is mixed with water and left in a covered, heated, and greased earthen container to cook slowly.

West Bengal ghotis are known for their pulipitha, which is usually made on the last day of Poush, the ninth month in the Bengali calendar that marks the beginning of the winter. It is extremely tedious to prepare and cannot be made without date palm jaggery. The pulipitha is made with the cream of wheat, ground coconut, sugar, full cream milk, and solid jaggery which is crushed along with cardamom for flavour. The puli or shell is made by boiling the cream of wheat in water. The cream of wheat absorbs all the water and becomes a big lump which is then mashed and made into little balls of dough, each ball then flattened and the sweetened coconut mixture put in the middle with the shell closed to form cylindrical rolls that taper towards the end. These pulis are then boiled in thickened reduced milk and the milk is flavoured with more crushed jaggery. Pulipitha is served slightly warm.

Odisha, always stealing Bengal's thunder, has its own plethora of pithas. The poda pitha is considered to be a favourite of Lord Jagannath's and is served during the Raja festival. The Raja festival needs a special mention because it's a three-day festival that pays tribute to the menstruation cycle. It is believed that the goddess Vasumati started menstruating during this time and that Mother Earth menstruates on these three days, and so a ceremonial bath takes place on the fourth day. The festival takes place each year in the Odia month of Asadha in mid-June. A major agrarian festival, it is celebrated predominantly across the coastal districts of Odisha. Women are not allowed to work during this period and spend the three days enjoying the festivities.

The poda pitha is made with a batter of ground black gram, rice, and coconut, and has a cake-like texture. The enduri pitha is a slightly more healthy pitha in which a turmeric leaf is filled with a sweet coconut stuffing and steamed. The Chitau Amabasya festival dedicated to Lord Jagannath, which falls on the night of the new moon in the month of Shravana (August), has its own pitha preparation. After a special ritual, the chitau pitha is prepared using rice flour and grated coconut—what is unique is that only one side of the pitha is cooked properly while the other side is cooked by the steam and heat in the vessel.

An interesting and extremely healthy sweetmeat is prepared in Odisha on the Hindu new year, Makar Sankranti, as well. The makar chaula is made with uncooked crushed rice which is freshly harvested and mixed with fruits like banana, grated coconut, apple, and sugar or jaggery. Diwali has its own Odia sweetmeat: the ghoda mithei, which is most commonly found on the streets of Cuttack. Sugar syrup and crystallized sugar is used to form sweets shaped like humans, horses, and elephants.

Another sweet associated with a religious ceremony, a prasad

I encountered when I shifted to Delhi and would keep hearing paeans to, was the kada prasad. This is usually prepared and served by the Sikh community during Navratri and even during Baisakhi or Lohri. At this time, gurdwaras serve halwa as 'kada prasad'—interestingly one has to recite the five baanis, or prayers that signify a commitment to the Sikh guru, while cooking kada prasad in the gurudwara's langar. While the kitchens of these gurudwaras serve other sweets as well, such as a sheera which is a halwa made with semolina, and jalebis, kada prasad is the most common. Kada prasad is made with wholewheat flour and cooked with ghee. A sugar syrup is prepared separately and the boiling hot syrup is poured into a mixture and cooked till it attains a homogenous dark brown, grainy consistency.

At the same time as Makar Sankranti, if you move towards southern India, in Tamil Nadu you will experience the festival of Pongal—a celebration of the sun god Surya. Almost all Tamil homes I know, even the most cosmopolitan ones, prepare a sweet pongal known as sakkarai pongal in Tamil. The sakkarai pongal is almost like a sweet porridge made with rice and dal, and flavoured with cardamoms and dry fruits. Another version of the sweet pongal is the shakkara pongal which is made with mishri or rock sugar.

The Parsis have their own smorgasbord of sweets prepared during the Parsi new year, Navroz. And I'd be remiss not to mention these, given that they can't be found easily in sweet shops—khaman na ladoo, or cornflour dumplings stuffed with sweetened coconut along with almonds and raisins; kopra pak, or coconut fudge; varadh vara, or semolina cakes; audh, a sweet made from coconut milk; and ariso, a milk and nut sweetmeat. Parsi sev is a version of the Muslim seviyan, and is prepared by sauteing vermicelli in butter and then adding sweetened milk with rose water and dry fruits, nutmeg, and cardamom. The vermicelli soaks up all the milk—which is when it is ready to be served.

Another fascinating sweet dish is prepared by the Bohri community. Malai na khaja, which is a layered, flaky, deep-fried pastry dipped in sugar syrup, is very similar to the baklava and possibly has Iranian roots. The Malido, which is very similar to the dimer halwa, is made from grains, nuts, dried fruits, and eggs and must be constantly stirred while being prepared till it is fudge-like.

My favourite though is the baked custard. One look at it and you know its British antecedents. The Parsi version includes rose water, cardamom, nutmeg, and flaked almonds. It's like a caramel custard paying homage to the country it now resides in.

These are just a pick of the many sweets which are prepared during religious festivals in India. There are many others, from the modaks and pedas made during Ganesh Chaturthi to the doodhiya kheench, a sweetened wheat porridge which is made in Rajasthan during the winter season and on Akshaya Tritiya. Or the dilkhusar or besan ki chakki, also known as mohanthal, which is made with coarsely ground gram flour, khoya, cardamom powder, sugar, milk, almonds, and ghee and cut into squares and served.

Religion might well be the opiate of the masses in India, but maybe the plethora of desserts offered in the name of religion have a role to play in it.

Acknowledgments

First on the list, I must thank Bena Sareen, my very dear friend and Aleph's talented book cover designer for recommending my name to the editor at Aleph when they thought of this book. And of course my editor, Simar, who was patience personified, and who handed me over to the editorial team at Aleph. I also want to thank Paul Beckett and Will Davies for allowing me to write on food in India for three years at the *Wall Street Journal* and showing me what good editing is and what fun food writing can be.

To my grandmother who loved cooking and hosting dinners, trying out new recipes, and instilling a similar love in me once I grew up—Brown Sahib would not have been possible without your genes and neither would this book have transpired.

The pandemic must be thanked for putting a spanner in

the works and delaying the book by almost a year, to the point that I was starting to forget what I'd written on. And my friends who've kept me in good cheer, not just in the last two years but also for as long as I've known them, and have rolled their eyes at me writing on Indian sweets, since they know I prefer a pastry to a pantua—Durga, Anu, Bini, Abhinandan, Sandip, Vishnu, Anindo, and everyone else who mocked me. A good mood helps one write better. And sarcastic and cruel friends are great motivators.

Thank you to all the sweetshops in Bengal. And the portly Indian who makes me believe that of course people love sweets, eating them, and reading about them. I also discovered that it was shocking that there is no one book which has been written about the cultural or historical influences on sweets in India, so my absolute gratitude to the writers and culinary historians who have written on one sweet or one community's specific delicacy or the other. If it wasn't for their work, I would be totally at sea trying to compile this book which I hope will be a little footnote in the culinary historical writing of India.

And last, but not least, thank you to my biggest critic and biggest support who painstakingly went through each chapter and pointed out—quite gleefully I must say—my incorrect grammar and fictional 'facts'. I think I've said it enough, but I appreciate each second you spared to wade through each chapter.

Recommended Reading

While writing this book, I referred to a number of books, papers, newspaper reports, and interviews of food historians—all of which are available in the public domain. I still didn't chance upon even one consolidated history of Indian sweets. The books, papers, and reports listed below have been referred to by me, and some are simply a delight to read, like the *Larousse Gastronomique* and *India: A Cookbook* which I've referred to often while trying to whip up something in the kitchen. My utter gratitude to all these writers and food historians who have done such remarkable work in studying and chronicling all things culinary.

Achaya, K. T., *Indian Food: A Historical Companion*, New Delhi: Oxford University Press, 1994.

Banerji, Chitrita, *Life and Food in Bengal*, New Delhi: Penguin

India, 2005.

Chatterjee, Priyadarshini, 'Why the sandesh is the perfect representation of cultural reforms in 19th-century Calcutta', *Scroll.in*, 16 August 2018.

Collingham, Lizzie, *Curry: A Tale of Cooks and Conquerors*, New York: Oxford University Press, 2007.

Dasgupta, Minakshie, Gupta, Bunny and Chaliha, Jaya, *The Calcutta Cookbook: A Treasury of Over 200 Recipes from Pavement to Palace*, New Delhi: Penguin Books India, 1995.

Dash, Madhulika, 'Culinary history: A journey called Daulat Ki Chaat', *bawarchi.com*, 7 October 2021.

Davidson, Alan, *The Oxford Companion to Food*, edited by Tom Jaine, New York: Oxford University Press, 2006.

de Silva Gracias, Fatima, *Cozinha de Goa*, Goa: Golden Heart Emporium Books, 2012.

Ghose, Amita, 'The rosogolla's bittersweet beginning: How a Calcutta confectioner created the dessert', *Firstpost*, 19 November 2017.

Krondl, Michael, *Sweet Invention: A History of Dessert*, Chicago: Chicago Review Press, 2011.

Mamgain, Asheesh, 'Sandesh to Ledikeni (Named After Lady Canning) Delhi Does Bengali Sweets Proud', *The Citizen*, 26 September 2018.

——, 'If You Could Eat the Clouds... It Would Be Nimish/Daulat ki Chaat', *The Citizen*, 4 January 2019.

Menezes, Vivek, 'Goa's Best Chef is a Secret', *Livemint*, 18 January 2020.

Montagn., Prosper, *Larousse Gastronomique*, edited by Robert J. Courtine, London: Hamlyn, 1988.

Muhammad ibn al-Hasan Ibn al-Karim, *A Baghdad Cookery Book: The Book of Dishes (Kitab al-Tabikh)*, Translated by Charles Perry, London: Prospect Books, 2005.

Padgaonkar, Dileep, 'Journey of the jalebi', *Times of India*, 15 March 2010.

Pant, Pushpesh, *India: Cookbook*, London: Phaidon, 2010.

Prajapati, J. B. and Nair, Baboo M., 'History of fermented foods', edited by E. R. Farnworth, *Handbook of Fermented Functional Foods (Functional Foods and Nutraceuticals)*, Florida: CRC Press, 2003.

Qarni, Owais, 'From royals to masses, few can resist Khushabi dhodha', *Express Tribune*, 3 February 2019.

Rajagopalan, Ashwin, 'Why Bebinca is Known as the Queen of Goan Desserts', *NDTV Food*, 18 May 2016.

Sharma, Chandni, 'How Do You Like Your Daulat Ki Chaat– Old School or High Tech?', *The Quint*, 16 October 2018.

Taylor Sen, Colleen, *Feasts and Fasts: A History of Food in India*, London: Reaktion Books, 2014.

Wahab, Amer, 'A brief introduction to Bengal's gastronomic history', *Daily Star*, 24 February 2020.